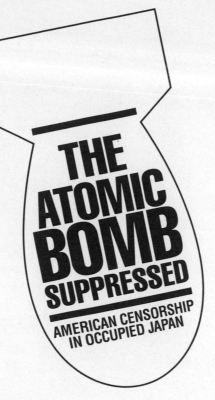

THE
ATOMIC
BOMB
SUPPRESSED

AMERICAN CENSORSHIP
IN OCCUPIED JAPAN

THE ATOMIC BOMB
VOICES FROM HIROSHIMA AND NAGASAKI
Edited and translated by Kyoko and Mark Selden

JAPAN'S NEW IMPERIALISM
Rob Steven

THE ATOMIC BOMB SUPPRESSED
AMERICAN CENSORSHIP IN OCCUPIED JAPAN
Monica Braw

JAPANESE WOMEN WRITERS
TWENTIETH CENTURY SHORT FICTION
*Edited and translated by Noriko Mizuta Lippit
and Kyoko Iriye Selden*

Asia and The Pacific

MONICA
BRAW

THE
ATOMIC
BOMB
SUPPRESSED

AMERICAN CENSORSHIP
IN OCCUPIED JAPAN

An East Gate Book
M. E. Sharpe, Inc.
Armonk, New York
London, England

An East Gate Book

Copyright © 1991 by M. E. Sharpe, Inc.

Library of Congress Cataloging-in-Publication Data

Braw, Monica.
    The atomic bomb suppressed: American censorship in occupied Japan
/ by Monica Braw.
      p. cm.—(Asia and the Pacific)
    Includes bibliographical references and index.
    ISBN 0-87332-628-8
    1. Press—Japan. 2. Freedom of the press—Japan. 3. Atomic bomb—Japan.
4. Japan—History—Allied occupation, 1945–1952. I. Title. II. Series: Asia and the
Pacific (Armonk, N.Y.)
PN5404.B7   1991
303.3′76—dc20   90-26811
                                                          CIP

Printed in the United States of America

TS   10 9 8 7 6 5 4 3 2 1

CONTENTS

FIGURES

PREFACE

Mark Selden

IN THE SUMMER of 1945, its World War II triumph capped by the atomic bombing of Hiroshima and Nagasaki, the United States set out to remake a defeated Japan in its own self-image as a free, democratic, and capitalist society. The occupation has been widely regarded as a rare success in the annals of war and peaceful transition: in just six years, the United States planted the seeds of a lasting democratic polity, assisted a ravaged economy to rapid recovery, paving the way for its subsequent emergence as an economic superpower, and restored Japanese sovereignty.

In this carefully researched and nuanced work, Monica Braw draws on declassified U.S. archives and on interviews with atomic victims and Japanese authorities to raise troubling questions about censorship and free speech, about atomic diplomacy, and about U.S. occupation policy, questions that prompt us to rethink central presuppositions of the postwar global order.

At the very moment that the United States was destroying the apparatus of censorship and repression of the Japanese imperial state, dismantling the giant zaibatsu firms that it pinpointed as the economic roots of fascism, and proclaiming its commitment to democratic and constitutional rule, the occupation authorities, under the direction of General Douglas MacArthur, implemented secret mechanisms of censorship. U.S. censors set out to mold Japanese public opinion, to shield the United States from public criticism, and to preserve a U.S. monopoly on information pertaining to the effects of the atomic bomb on its victims.

This study details the inner workings of the U.S. censorship apparatus as it pertained to the atomic bombing of Japan and assesses the manifold consequences for Japanese democracy, for the United States as a global power, for world peace, and for the victims of the bomb. It shows how U.S. censors implemented comprehensive censorship and postcensorship controls on the Japanese press and banned literary works, including novels, poetry, and children's stories, as well as films that explored the troubling issues of atomic destruction. In one extraordinary case that reached the highest echelons of occupation censorship, General Charles Willoughby first denied and later permitted publication of the personal account of the Catholic Doctor Nagai Takasi, but only on condition that *The Bells Toll for Nagasaki* be published together with an account of Japanese atrocities in the Philippines. The result was the unwitting tacit admission that the dropping of the atomic bombs on Japanese civilians was the moral equivalent of Japanese wartime atrocities. Even as their own censorship mechanisms were being set in place, the U.S. authorities wrote into Japan's new constitution (Article 21) that ''No censorship shall be maintained . . .''

Braw's evenhanded treatment of censorship issues reveals deep and persistent divisions within the occupation over issues of censorship in general and atomic censorship in particular. If the system was far from monolithic, this study nevertheless shows that censorship:

—distorted the postwar global nuclear debate by stilling the voices of atomic victims and by concealing basic information on the consequences of atomic warfare in general and radiation in particular;

—impeded the treatment of atomic vicims by emphasizing secrecy and barring dissemination of medical research results, approaches geared to preserving U.S. nuclear supremacy rather than to aiding victims;

—shaped the course of postwar Japanese politics and consciousness by denying victims and critics of the bomb an arena to air their grievances, and by establishing a duplicitous standard for a democratic polity.

Monica Braw, historian, investigative journalist, and novelist, brings to this study insights that contribute to the continuing global debate over nuclear war, the global role of the United States, and the nature of democratic transitions.

ABBREVIATIONS

ABCC	Atomic Bomb Casualty Commission
AEC	Atomic Energy Commission
AFPAC	Armed Forces Pacific
AFSWP	Armed Forces Southwest Pacific
ASF	Armed Service Forces
CCD	Civil Censorship Detachment (SCAP)
CCS	Combined Chiefs of Staff
CIC	Counter-Intelligence Corps Detachment (SCAP)
CIE	Civil Information and Education Section (SCAP)
CIS	Civil Intelligence Section (SCAP)
ESS	Economic and Scientific Section (SCAP)
FEC	Far Eastern Commission
G-2	Intelligence Section; Head of Intelligence Section (GHQ)
GHQ	General Headquarters (SCAP); especially in Japanese used synonymously with SCAP
JCAC	Joint (Army and Navy) Civil Affairs Committee
JCS	Joint Chiefs of Staff
JIC	Joint Intelligence Committee
MED	Manhattan Engineering District
MLC	Military Liaison Committee (AEC to JCS)
OCCI	Office of Chief of Counter-Intelligence (SCAP)
OSRD	Office of Scientific Research and Development
OSS	Office of Strategic Services

POLAD   Political Adviser to SCAP (State Department)
PPB   Press, Pictorial and Broadcast Section (SCAP)
PPS   Policy Planning Staff, Department of State
RG   Record Group, United States National
                 Archives
SCAP   Supreme Commander for the Allied Powers
                 (Commonly used to refer both to General
                 Douglas MacArthur, who held the position of
                 SCAP, and to the Occupation authorities in
                 general. See also GHQ.)
SPU   Special Projects Unit, ESS, SCAP
SWNCC   State-War-Navy Coordinating Committee

ACKNOWLEDGMENTS
TO THE SECOND EDITION

THE FIRST edition of *The Atomic Bomb Suppressed* was published as a doctoral dissertation at the University of Lund, Sweden. For this second, revised edition I have incorporated research and information that has been brought to my attention since 1986 and omitted some parts to make the book more accessible to the reader.

For ideas, discussions, information, and support in this work I would especially like to thank Mark Selden as well as Anita O'Brien of M. E. Sharpe. Seiitsu Tachibana, who translated *The Atomic Bomb Suppressed* into Japanese, has contributed improvements and additional information. The Japanese Association of Occupation Policy Studies again provided me with new knowledge. Jussi remains cheerful and critical in addition to sharing his computer.

Tokyo
November 27, 1990

ACKNOWLEDGMENTS

MANY people in several countries have helped me and encouraged me in this work, which has stretched from Sweden to Japan and onward to the United States. My greatest debt is to all those survivors of the atomic bombs who still live in Hiroshima and Nagasaki and untiringly try to tell the world about their experiences. I would especially like to mention Professor Shigetoshi Iwamatsu of Nagasaki and Professor Seiji Imahori of Hiroshima. I have had rewarding contacts with the Japanese Association of Occupation Policy Studies, where particularly Professor Akira Amakawa has shown interest in my work. Professor Jun Eto kindly shared much of his extensive material on Occupation censorship. I would also like to thank Takeshi Maezawa of Yomiuri Shimbun and Mitsuo Nitta of Yushodo Booksellers.

In the United States, Dr. Wilcomb E. Washburn provided many useful introductions. At the National Archives, especially Edward Reese and John E. Taylor led me to invaluable documents. At the Gordon W. Prange Collection of Maryland University, Frank Shulman and Eizaburo Okuizumi introduced me to important material. Professor Marlene E. Mayo discussed Occupation policies, and the late Professor Gordon W. Prange, although already very ill, answered my questions.

In Sweden, I particularly want to thank my university teacher from the earliest years, Lars-Arne Norborg, for the enthusiasm toward the study of history that he has always imparted. The late Gertrud Brundin, editor-in-chief of the Science and Research Department of the Swedish Radio Company, encouraged me and gave me opportunities to combine work and study. My brother

Christian has given me much asked-for advice. At the Department of History at the University of Lund, Leif Eliasson and Tulli Agrell arranged for all that I needed, although I have often been very far away. Britt Hörnstedt has given unfailing support and also spread the fruits of this work to the general public as part of peace education within ABF/TBV (Swedish Workers'/Civil Servants' Study Organizations). A grant from the Peace Foundation of the Swedish Foreign Ministry made possible an abridged and popularized version of this work in Swedish.

For the scrutiny of my English and other comments I am grateful to Chris Kleemeier and Barbara Yates. Aki Takayanagi was absolutely tireless and indispensable in helping me with word processing. Motohiko Hirao of Rapid Printing has also taken a great interest in my work and enlightened me further about the work of a mail censor during the American Occupation.

Last, but certainly not least, my professor and adviser Göran Rystad has led me forward with countless letters containing advice, photocopies, contacts, and books. My father Lars Braw has been a tireless supporter in word and deed, from the beginning making me believe that I could do anything. My husband Juhani Lompolo has participated in my efforts with cheer and criticism.

Tokyo
February 19, 1986

THE
ATOMIC
BOMB
SUPPRESSED

AMERICAN CENSORSHIP
IN OCCUPIED JAPAN

1

INTRODUCTION

FORTY-FIVE years after the atomic bombs that destroyed Hiroshima and Nagasaki in August 1945, the world abounds with
material about the consequences of nuclear weapons. We are not
only familiar with the fact that nuclear weapons are directed at
major cities all over the world and that new "devices" are con-
tinually installed, but we also realize the indescribable results if
these weapons were ever used. We have heard about "nuclear
winter," which would leave no environment suitable for human
life, and about the neutron bomb, which would leave buildings
but no life.

In comparison, the atomic bombs of Hiroshima and Nagasaki
were ridiculously small. They affected less than half a million
people. Today, the cities destroyed are sprawling centers where
one has to search for signs of catastrophe. Every visitor who
comes to Hiroshima and Nagasaki for the first time is surprised,
and perhaps also, for at least a moment, inclined to doubt the
horrors that were so real forty-five years ago. But those horrors
still haunt the survivors as nightmares about the past and as fear
for the future and the health of unborn generations.

The survivors of Hiroshima and Nagasaki are still the only
human beings who can tell what it means to survive nuclear war.
In spite of that, the world has only occasionally listened to them.
In fact, only periodically has the world concerned itself with the
effects of nuclear weapons at all. Today, we live in times when

this concern is widespread, but this was not so in 1969. Then it was possible for a young Swedish woman like myself to arrive in Hiroshima and be shocked that I had realized so little of what the atomic bombing of Hiroshima means. I was shaken by my own lack of realization and by the sorrow of the survivors at not being heard.

I thought at that time that it was solely out of disinterest and inertia that Hiroshima and Nagasaki were not on the minds of people in general. I could find no explanation as to why the atomic bombings received mere passing mention in the history books of my native Sweden. But being a writer, I wanted to remedy this lack of knowledge as best as I could by interviewing survivors and publishing their stories.

I soon became aware, however, that it had not always been possible to conduct such interviews, much less to publish them. Many of the *hibakusha* (atomic bomb survivors) I met told me that material about the atomic bomb, its effects, and the conditions of hibakusha in Hiroshima and Nagasaki had been censored. One of them was Issei Nishimori, a medical doctor who specialized in pathology, particularly white corpuscle count in the blood. He was a medical student at the time of the atomic bombing of Nagasaki. After the war he decided to concentrate on research concerning the effects of the atomic bomb on human beings. But he soon discovered that this was very difficult:

> Partly this was because we could not afford research. We had to make a living. But partly it was because if we had conducted research we would not have been able to make the results public. Research during this period soon after the actual bombings would have been important. The Americans did not order us to stop, but they imposed so many restrictions, for example, that everything had to be translated into English, that in practice we were prohibited from publishing.
>
> Also, they took all the autopsy material that we had collected and sent it to America. Had even half of it been left, we pathologists could have done research on the effects of the atomic bomb on

human beings. As it was, there was no autopsy material about the important period of the bombing and its immediate aftermath. The material was not returned to us for thirty years, and then only after we repeatedly asked for it. At that time, of course, it was already history.

Neither were we told anything about the results of the research undertaken at the Atomic Bomb Casualty Commission (ABCC), started in Hiroshima in 1947. All results were sent to America. There was no possibility of having them published in Japan. In addition, the ABCC only did research. It did not try to cure. It kept many secrets. This made hibakusha feel that they were experimental animals. As a doctor I think it is common sense that when one finds something new during research one should publish it for the benefit of all human beings. But the ABCC did not share its research. Had the Americans, with their higher knowledge in medical science, done that, many patients would have been saved.[1]

Another person who told me about limits to the spread of information about the atomic bombings was Sueo Inoue, a cameraman for Nippon Eiga-sha (Nippon Film Co.) In September 1945 he had been sent to Hiroshima and Nagasaki to film the destruction:

Our plan was to appeal against the inhumanity of the atomic bomb to the Red Cross in Geneva. Our team also belonged to an academic investigation group doing research about the effects of the bomb. We were thirty-two or thirty-three persons. On September 16 we started filming in Nagasaki. We continued until October 24, when we were arrested by American military police. Then all work was stopped. All the film was confiscated. I was told to return to Tokyo.

My company protested against the confiscation, but we were told that it was on orders from the American Navy. When the Americans watched our films, they found them useful. So they changed our orders and gave us permission to take more film. We had finished in Hiroshima but returned to Nagasaki. By December we had completed our work. Then we were ordered to edit the films. The films were taken to America—everything we had shot and edited, even the small cuts. All in all it was 30,000 feet of film. The Japanese government had to pay the cost of the raw film.

But secretly we copied some film before giving it to the Americans. Only four people knew about this film. If the Occupation authorities had known, they would probably have sent us to Okinawa for hard labor. The reason we made the copy was that we wanted to show proof of the inhumanity of the atomic bomb. We wanted to send the film to the Red Cross in Geneva. But under the Occupation we did not dare to. We thought maybe we would be able to show it when the Occupation had come to an end.[2]

Even people who had nothing to do with information, newspapers, or film-making knew about restrictions. Tsukasa Uchida was a Nagasaki schoolboy in 1945:

The Americans brought bulldozers to clear up the Urakami area which had been hit by the atomic bomb. There were still many dead under the rubbish. Despite that the Americans drove their bulldozers very fast, treating the bones of the dead just the same as sand or soil. They carried the soil to lower places and used it to broaden roads there. A person who tried to take a picture of what they were doing was approached by the military police. The MP pointed his gun and threatened to confiscate any picture taken.

Because of the Press Code there was no possibility for us to write about such incidents. Newspapermen did not tell about them and they did not appear even in the readers' columns.

But Dr. Takashi Nagai was allowed to publish what he wrote. He was a Catholic. He called the atomic bomb a kind of baptism. In spite of the horrendous conditions after the bombing in Nagasaki he said that God must have had a special meaning, letting the atomic bomb be dropped on the Urakami area, where many Catholics lived.[3]

Hideo Matsuno, who was a journalist at the Domei News Agency, told me: "Because of the Press Code, we could not write freely. I kept my reports about Nagasaki in the hope that someday I would be able to publish them."[4]

In Hiroshima I was told similar things by the poet Sadako Kurihara. During our interview she suddenly said: "We could never have written about our experiences of the atomic bomb during the Occupation. It would have been impossible because of the censorship."[5]

Like most other people, I never thought of censorship in connection with the American Occupation of Japan. I had read many histories about this period and never heard about censorship. I associated censorship with dictatorship. The Occupation, on the other hand, I thought of as the democratization of defeated, militaristic Japan. "We were not allowed to write about the atomic bomb during the Occupation. We were not even allowed to say that we were not allowed to write about the atomic bomb," Ms. Kurihara explained.

Why? From those days in the 1970s when I first heard about Occupation censorship, I wanted to find the answer. But when I looked through available literature about the Occupation, I rarely found censorship mentioned, and then most often in passing. Regarding censorship of the atomic bomb, there were only brief reminiscences by people like Sadako Kurihara, who had themselves experienced it.

In 1977 the United States declassified the archives on the Occupation of Japan. The complete *Records of the Supreme Commander for the Allied Forces*, with a few exceptions, became available to the public. This enormous collection of material, although extremely poorly organized, opened up completely new possibilities for research into one of the most extensive attempts at social engineering ever—the remaking of Japan in the image of American democracy.

For the first time it also became possible extensively to research censorship during the American Occupation. No comprehensive studies on this subject had been written before that. The transformation of the minds and hearts of the Japanese people through the activities of the Civil Information and Education Section of the Occupation authorities have been studied— for example, the reformation of the education system. The censorship operations, on the other hand, were left largely unresearched, although they certainly played an important part in influencing Japanese knowledge and opinions. Because of this, when I started studying censorship of the atomic bomb I first had to find out about censorship in general.

My first question was: Why did the American Occupation impose censorship at all? Why and how was it decided to introduce censorship? Wasn't censorship totally inimical to the concept of democracy? Introducing democracy to Japan was the stated aim of the Allies. I could understand that censorship might be necessary when troops are occupying enemy territory in war. But Japan was not exclusively regarded as a defeated enemy after the surrender; it was a nation earmarked to become "better." The Japanese were to discard the military beliefs that led to war, in favor of democracy, which would assure peace. That, in short, was the American agenda. With that starting point, was the censorship envisaged as a military operation? Or did it in practice become something other than planned? How did the United States and the other Allies reason?

When I started studying the censorship plans I soon understood that the censorship operations were very broad. Generally speaking, Japan was an unknown country for Americans, even if Japan specialists in different departments prepared wide-ranging reports.[6] For the ordinary participant in the Occupation, it was not only Japan's culture that was unknown. Even more important, from the viewpoint of censorship, was that few Americans understood the Japanese language, and it was extremely difficult to learn. How could censorship be feasible under such circumstances? Who were the censors? How did they work?

The practical aspects aside, what did the censors censor? The first thing that comes to mind is that censors delete criticism of themselves and the rulers they represent. Was this the case in Japan, in spite of the basic premises of democracy, which allow free political discussion? How was it possible under such circumstances to draw lines for what to allow and what to ban? Without clear-cut restrictions, could censorship be effective?

Not until these questions were answered would it be possible to take up the case of censorship of atomic bomb material. Dr. Nishimori, Mr. Inoue, Mr. Uchida, Mr. Matsuno, and Ms.

Kurihara had stated that they had not been allowed to write freely about the atomic bomb. In spite of that, a look at bibliographies of books published during the Occupation showed that some works had been published on that subject. How was that possible? I had to ask: Were the Japanese I interviewed wrong?

The rules of American censorship, the Press Code, made no mention of the atomic bomb. In fact, the rules were rather vague. But when I found reports of censorship written by censors themselves it became clear that much material about the atomic bomb had, indeed, been censored. What was allowed and what was prohibited? With what motivations? And, above all, where were those decisions made? Was censorship policy in Japan concerning the atomic bomb set locally or in Washington? What were the reasons for censoring such material? It was, after all, already known throughout the world that on August 6, 1945, Hiroshima was obliterated by such a bomb. Hiroshima and Nagasaki could hardly be said to be a secret. As a whole, I wanted to know the result of the censorship of the atomic bomb in Japan during the first four years after the atomic bombings of Hiroshima and Nagasaki.

These are questions that this study tries to answer. I have had to limit myself mainly to newspaper censorship, but I believe that this topic is representative of censorship in general. Further detailed studies are needed. I have searched the American archives of the Occupation to try to explain how the occupiers themselves reasoned and worked and to find the result of their actions. In doing so, it may seem that I have forgotten the hibakusha and their own evidence of what it was like to live under the Occupation and to write under censorship. But they are not forgotten. Had it not been for them, this study would never have been made. By making it I hope to contribute to an understanding of nuclear weapons, of their horror and their importance, both to those who possess them and to their victims.

2

THE ATOMIC BOMB
PRESENTED TO THE WORLD

ON AUGUST 6, 1945, an atomic bomb was detonated above the Japanese city of Hiroshima. That day in Washington President Harry Truman made an announcement:

> Sixteen hours ago an American airplane dropped one bomb on Hiroshima, an important Japanese army base. This bomb had more power than 20,000 tons of TNT. With this bomb we have now added a new and revolutionary increase in destruction to supplement the growing power of our armed forces. It is an atom bomb. It is a harnessing of the basic power of the universe. We are now prepared to obliterate more rapidly and completely every production enterprise the Japanese have above ground in any city. We shall destroy their docks, their factories and their communications. Let there be no mistake; we shall completely destroy Japan's power to make war. It was to spare the Japanese people from utter destruction that the ultimatum of July 26 was issued at Potsdam.[1]

The same day, still August 6 in the United States, the top news story was self-evident. The *Washington Daily News*, for instance, filled its first page with the headlines "ATOM BOMB HITS JAPAN Nip Base Gets First 'Tiny' Sample Equaling 20,000 Tons of TNT AND WORSE ONES ARE ON THE WAY." The *Daily Mirror* of New York covered its first page with the headline "ATOMIC BOMB ROCKS JAP CITY." In graphics the tremendous power of the hitherto completely unknown weapon was explained: "1 atom bomb equals 100 B-29's carrying 10 tons each of TNT.'' In a dispatch from Guam in the Pacific, United Press reported '' 'My God' says crew as flash wipes out 60 Pct. of Hiroshima.'' In another dispatch from Washington, D.C., the same news agency reported that the Allies were considering a new ultimatum calling on Japan to surrender or be annihilated by atomic power. During the days that followed, American newspapers were filled with items about the atomic bomb. There were reports about conditions in Hiroshima and, later, Nagasaki. There were also editorial comments and opinions from the readers. Many were horrified and warned about the consequences for the future.[2]

In Japan the situation was very different. Hiroshima was practically obliterated, but nobody, save those who were there, knew. The first reports reached Tokyo about noon, some four hours after the explosion. They were from the Japanese news agency Domei, which managed to send a telegram from the vicinity.[3] In the afternoon the managing editors of Domei and of the five big Tokyo newspapers were called to the Information and Intelligence Agency, the government office in charge of censorship. They were told that the information about what had happened in Hiroshima was inadequate, and that they should bury the news of the bombing in some obscure place, so that it seemed like an ordinary air raid.[4]

As a result, on the morning after the atomic bombing of Hiroshima one of Japan's largest newspapers, *Asahi shimbun*, carried the news in a story headlined "Small and Medium Cities Attacked by 400 B-29's." The last four lines of the article read: "Hiroshima was attacked by incendiary bombs. . . . It seems that some damage was caused to the city and its vicinity."[5]

Meanwhile, the government had received more detailed reports in an official telegram from the superintendent general of the Chugoku district (where Hiroshima is situated). He told of appalling damage by a new type of bomb. At dawn on August 7 another report arrived, this time containing the statement: "The whole city of Hiroshima was destroyed instantly by a single bomb."[6]

In the afternoon the Imperial Headquarters finally released an official communiqué saying that considerable damage had been caused to Hiroshima in an attack by a small number of B-29's, and that a new type of bomb was used. As for details, it mentioned that a considerable number of houses collapsed but said nothing about the 100,000 and more killed and maimed, and nothing about the appalling conditions that reigned in the city. As an afterthought it cautioned that the new type bomb "should not be made light of."[7]

The government received further reports of the damage from Professor Yoshio Nishina, Japan's leading nuclear physicist and the head of its own atomic bomb project at the Riken Institute. Nishina had been sent to Hiroshima to assess the damage. His report to the government on August 8 stated:

> What I've seen so far is unspeakable. Tens of thousands dead. Bodies piled up everywhere. Sick, wounded, naked people wandering around in a daze. . . . Almost no buildings left standing.
> It's all true then? Hiroshima is completely wiped out? Completely. . . . I'm very sorry to tell you this . . . the so-called new-type bomb is actually an atomic bomb.[8]

Newspaper reports during the next few days did not reflect the news from Professor Nishina. On August 9, *Asahi* published the first announcement by Air Defense Headquarters. It contained warnings of the blast and of thermal heat of the "new-type bomb." But it also recommended countermeasures, such as reducing the exposed part of the body and taking care to extinguish open flames in the kitchen when evacuating. In a third announcement published two days later, the Headquarters recommended that "white underwear is effective for protection against burns." The bomb was not referred to as an atomic bomb. Instead, attempts were made to belittle the importance of the bomb, as in the lead article in *Asahi* on August 9, which said that "the power of new types of offensive weapons to appear during the course of war is in many cases greatly exaggerated." The next day an officer who had been in Hiroshima was quoted as saying, "A bomb of this level is already in the process of being tested in our country, too . . . the new-type bomb is hardly something beyond what we could imagine."[9]

These reports appeared in the middle of hardship that struck everyone. Almost all cities and towns were subject to air raids, food was scarce, and people were exhausted just trying to live. Those who had survived Hiroshima were mostly too injured or shocked to travel. Thus, it was not until the morning of August 9 that nine persons, using whatever strength and ingenuity they had left, managed to reach Nagasaki where they had family, friends, or other connections. One of them, a newspaper publisher, gathered courage on arrival in Nagasaki and informed the prefectural governor of the disaster in Hiroshima. Well aware that he was liable to be accused of the crime of spreading rumors and endangering public security, he asked the governor not to repeat his story to anyone. The governor nevertheless assembled executives of the municipal government in a big bomb shelter and informed them.[10] On the morning of August 9, the Nagasaki authorities themselves had had the first direct contacts with Hiroshima after the atomic bombing. But they were more concerned with another catastrophe, which seemed to be of much greater consequence. The telegraphic communications from the Japanese puppet state Manchukuo reached Nagasaki before they were forwarded to Tokyo. Thus it was the Nagasaki authorities who were the first to learn the feared news that the Soviet Union had declared war on Japan and that Soviet troops had already crossed the border into Manchuria. Japan now faced one more powerful enemy.

So it happened that when the second atomic bomb was dropped on Nagasaki the authorities, and certainly the inhabitants, were almost as ignorant about what had occurred as those in Hiroshima had been three days earlier.[11]

After the bombing of Nagasaki, the press continued to publish encouraging reports. Three journalists from *Asahi* were sent to Hiroshima and reported on August 12 on the devastation they found there. The headline read "Hiroshima Transformed Instantaneously." They described how "Hiroshima was for the most part reduced to ashes and a large number of innocent people were killed or injured." But the reason for the destruction, they said, was not so much the new-type bomb itself as "unfamiliarity" with it. Their report ended: "We cannot even dream of the Japanese race losing the will to fight just because of this." In a similar vein, a nuclear physicist, Dr. Koji Fushimi, was interviewed on August 10 in *Asahi*. He assured that "there is absolutely no reason to fear the new-type bomb." One way to be "absolutely safe" from exposure to thermal rays was to refrain from wearing short-sleeved shirts and shorts. Several reports endorsed preparations for living underground.[12]

In Washington there were worries that the Japanese might not fully understand their situation. In a message to Secretary of War Henry L. Stimson, Secretary of State James F. Byrnes wrote that it did not seem the Japanese government had informed the people of the Allied surrender offer in July, and that a leaflet raid ought to be carried out over the Japanese islands.[13] The secretary of war was able to inform him that such plans were already under way: the day after the Hiroshima bombing, the War Department had sent instructions on the matter to Brigadier General T. F. Farrell, deputy head of the Manhattan Project and top man in the field, responsible for the atomic bomb team on Tinian in the Pacific. In addition to radio transmissions, the plan included the dropping of sixteen million leaflets and half a million newspapers containing stories and pictures of the atomic bomb strike.[14] To prepare such material took time, however, and the propaganda raids over Japanese cities did not start until August 13.[15]

After August 9 and the Soviet declaration of war, the government and the military in Tokyo spent endless inconclusive sessions trying to decide what to do. This confusion may have contributed to laxness in Japanese censorship.[16] In Nagasaki, where half the city was destroyed, it is doubtful if the local censors had any possibility of influencing the press. In any case, the damage was of course so obvious that the local surviving newspaper, *Nagasaki shimbun*, would not have been able to suppress news of the atomic bombing however harsh the censorship would otherwise have been. An attempt, surprisingly enough, was made the day after, on August 10, when the headline read: "Nagasaki City Hit by New-Type Bomb. Damages Estimated Slight." This article was accompanied by a statement from the Western Area Army stating that by decentralization and the construction of a huge caverned city it was possible to survive the new-type bomb.[17]

But publication of facts about the harsh living conditions in general and about the situation in Hiroshima and Nagasaki were also a result of explicit government policies. The United States Army Signal Intelligence Service, which had broken the secret Japanese code used by the Foreign Ministry to communicate with its legations abroad, kept a close watch via "Operation Magic" on everything that was transmitted through that channel. On August 15, the Foreign Ministry beamed out information about a cabinet decision concerning how to direct public opinion in view of the surrender. Apart from exhorting the people to brace themselves and to unite, the government had decided that "since things have turned out as they have, general anger, grief, and criticism are to be allowed." There were limits, however: Communistic and revolutionary social statements were to be dealt with effectively, and "any statements recommending direct action or statements full of desperation" were to be suitably controlled.[18]

Despite attempts to belittle the effects, the government accused the United States of cruelty and inhumanity for using the atomic bomb. In an official protest on August 12, which was sent via the Swiss Legation, the government described Hiroshima as a provincial town without any protection or special military installations of any kind. (In fact, it was the headquarters for the Western Area Army, and an important naval base was located close by in Kure.) The description of the atomic bomb was to the point: "a bomb having the most cruel effects humanity has ever known

. . . surpass[ing] by far gas or any other [kind of] arm[s] the use of which is prohibited by the treaties.''[19]

In *Asahi*, the Japanese could read the text of the protest, which said in part:

> It has been established on-the-scene that the damage extends over a great area and that combatant and noncombatant men and women, old and young, are massacred without discrimination by the blast of the explosion, as well as by the radiating heat which results therefrom. Accordingly, this bomb has the most cruel effects humanity has ever known . . .
>
> [The Americans] have shown complete defiance of the essential principles of humanitarian laws, as well as international law. They now use this new bomb, having uncontrollable and cruel effect much greater than any other arms or projectiles ever used to date. This constitutes a new crime against humanity and civilization.[20]

The protest was in line with earlier published announcements and criticism of the United States. In its initial announcement, the Imperial Headquarters on August 7 denounced the inhumanity of the atomic bomb: ''The enemy's use of this new-type bomb plainly reveals his brutal aim of shedding the innocent blood of civilians . . . the enemy, who dared such inhuman cruelty, should not for some time once again be able to utter the terms justice and humanity.'' On August 9 *Asahi* declared: ''The fact that the enemy is resorting to the violence of bombing the innocent masses while advocating justice and humanity has been finally made clear by the results of the survey [of Hiroshima].'' *Asahi* also published reports of European reactions to the use of the atomic bomb, quoting a Swedish newspaper that called the atomic bombings by the United States ''a truly inhuman, frightful thing.''[21] In a broadcast to the American zone the same day, Domei quoted the *Nippon Times* editorial of the same day. It said in part:

> Not only has the greater part of Hiroshima been wiped out, but an extraordinary proportion of the inhabitants has been either killed or injured. The use of a weapon of such terrifying destructiveness not

only commands attention as a matter of new technique in the conduct of war. More fundamentally and vitally it opens up a most grave and profound moral problem in which the very future of humanity is at stake.

The recent American attack on Hiroshima was an act of premeditated wholesale murder, the deliberate snuffing out of lives of tens of thousands of innocent civilians who had no chance of protecting themselves in the slightest degree.

It is not primarily a matter of legal justifiability or even of principles of international conduct. It is a matter that goes to the very heart of the fundamental concept of human morality.

How can a human being with any claim to a sense of moral responsibility deliberately let loose an instrument of destruction that can at one stroke annihilate an appalling segment of man kind? . . . This is a crime against god and humanity which strikes at the very basis of moral existence.

What meaning is there in any international law, in any rule of human conduct, in any concept of right and wrong, if the very foundations of morality are to be overthrown as this instrument of total destruction threatens to do?

On August 15 Emperor Hirohito finally spoke. That he would do so, over the radio, was something so unbelievable that, according to many recollections, some of those who were gathered around radio sets simply did not understand what he said. His stilted court language and the poor reception conditions contributed to the difficulties, of course, but the whole concept of the emperor telling the people that the war was over was so bewildering that many thought he called on them to fight on.

In his speech the emperor also touched on the atomic bombings. He said: ''Moreover the enemy has begun to employ a new and most cruel bomb, the power of which to do damage is indeed incalculable, taking the toll of many innocent lives. Should we continue to fight not only would it result in an ultimate collapse and the obliteration of the nation but also it would lead to total extinction of human civilization.''[22]

Immediately after the surrender, newspapers published many

articles on the conditions in both Hiroshima and Nagasaki. The first pictures were published in *Asahi* August 19 and 25. There were eyewitness accounts. The three reporters from *Asahi* wrote on August 23 that 90 percent of the buildings had been destroyed, there were 200,000 casualties, and even mosquitoes were totally wiped out. There was little optimism as to how one could protect oneself: "There was no time to evacuate nor time to extinguish flames. There was absolutely no time to put into effect the countermeasures already established for air defense or fire prevention." The details of the horrors were vivid:

> Although initially the number of dead was given as 10,000, the number increased with the passage of time and it is finally said to have reached 100,000. It can be imagined from this just how cruel the atomic bomb's power is. Moreover, as is usual with those who succumb to burns, the victims were fully conscious until their death. Those who were looking after the patients, who continued to scream out "kill me quickly," declared in unison, with a sense of anguish going straight to the bone, "it's a living hell on earth."

A reporter in Nagasaki wrote an article in the same issue of *Asahi* under the headline "Baked [to Death] in Air-Raid Shelters. 23,000 Dead or Missing." He described the victims:

> They are lying around in every conceivable place. Just their eyes are burning with indignation; their faces and bodies are covered with blood due to glass shards. They are groaning, their faces distorted, with the skin peeled off their faces due to being burned. Some, with half the body turned to skeleton, could at least be distinguished as to whether they are male or female. But that's all. You cannot tell who anyone is.[23]

Doctors and research teams reported their findings. There was frightening news about people dying who had seemed completely well and were without injuries. *Asahi* reported that two weeks after the bombings the death toll continued to rise, with the numbers of dead reaching sixty thousand on August 25, up from thirty thousand dead in the earlier reports. Dr. Masao Tsuzuki, head of the Department of Surgery of Tokyo Imperial University, was interviewed in *Asahi* August 29, after visiting Hiroshima. He told about "victims, who had suffered nothing more than a scratch at the time, lost their hair a few days later . . . and died." He thought that this was the effect of radiation: "We had originally thought that the range of [damage by] the atomic bomb was limited to two: destruction from blast and burns from thermal rays. It has now been proven that, in addition to these two, harmful after-effects also result from the action of 'radioactive particles.' "[24]

The discussion outside Japan about how the atomic bomb would influence the future of the world was reported. *Asahi* quoted a bishop's sermon severely criticizing "the inhumanity of the bomb." On September 12, an American soldier in Japan told an interviewer: "Even in the United States loud voices are being raised in criticism of the atomic bombings. They are saying that, if any bombs are left, they should be dumped into the Pacific Ocean."[25]

The comments of the American survey team that finally arrived were also reported. "Damages beyond imagination" was the quote (which later became a matter of investigation and denial on the American side).[26]

In transmissions abroad directed toward the United States, the central news agency Domei on August 25 quoted Tokyo newspapers. For the past week they were said to have featured "gripping pictures." The situation was completely indescribable, completely defying the most fantastic dreams of havoc. The next day Domei quoted an editorial in *Nippon Times* about the atomic bombing, saying that it "should shock even a world calloused by the unprecedented cruelty of the late worldwide war." It pointed to the moral problem, which it called a problem of paramount urgency. "Mankind must be spared from any possibility of a repetition of such suffering. . . . It is not a matter of statecraft; it is not even a matter of high ideals; it is a matter of simple humanitarianism."[27]

The time between the announcement of Japan's surrender on

August 15 and the actual signing of the surrender documents on September 2 aboard the U.S. warship *Missouri* in Tokyo Bay was a confusing period. Nobody in Japan, including the government and the military, really knew what was going to happen next. The press took the opportunity to demand less government control of the media. *Mainichi*, a leading newspaper, wrote: "One has the impression that official secrecy has almost become a habit—it can even be said that to thoroughly uproot that habit is one of the prerequisite conditions for the rehabilitation of the State today."[28] On August 28, the Cabinet Board of Information announced that controls on the press, which had been in force since 1937, would be removed. Until the Diet could revoke them, they would not be strictly enforced. The prime minister, Prince Higashikuni, said that freedom of speech would be recognized. The press greeted the announcement with satisfaction. *Yomiuri-Hoshi* wrote: "Now is the time when facts alone can be trusted." William Coughlin, an American journalist working in Japan during the Occupation, wrote that the press comments gave the impression that a tremendous resurgence of democratic feeling had seized a liberal press. But he cautioned that many associated with the newspapers, including the owners, had supported the militarists.[29]

In the confusion, the Japanese press experienced what would be its most extensive freedom until the end of 1949. The Japanese were unsure of their limits, but it seemed clear that the old rulers were out and that the new ones, the Americans, advocated democracy and liberalization. What that meant in practice, however, was not stated until September 18, when the Press Code came into force. How the Press Code worked became clear only gradually. That it would be used to promote not only the demilitarization and democratization of Japan but also the selfish interests of the United States, especially its concern to conceal information about the atomic bomb, was perhaps not evident from the beginning. But that was indeed the purpose for which it was extensively employed.

IDEALS AND GOALS OF U.S. OCCUPATION PLANNING AND CENSORSHIP

THE UNITED STATES started to plan for the Occupation of Japan at a time when most Americans and Europeans only dared hope that the war would end with an Allied victory. The planning was done within different departments and interested both the military and civilians. It was also subject to civilian and military contacts between the Allies, but when the Japanese surrender finally came, only the United States had concrete plans.[1]

Detailed planning, including discussions on censorship, got underway in the summer of 1943.[2] At a meeting of the Allied Combined Chiefs of Staff a censorship plan for Europe and North Africa had been approved, and planning for the Asia-Pacific Area was being undertaken by the War Department in cooperation with the Navy Department.[3] The War and Navy departments were assisted by the director of the U.S. Office of Censorship, Byron Price, who had initiated a correspondence with Secretary of War Henry Stimson on these questions. In a letter to Price on September 29, 1943, Stimson explained what was happening in the area of censorship planning.[4] In addition, Price corresponded with the Department of State, which told him that primary responsibility for censorship in captured or occupied territory belonged to the War Department, but that other departments would be kept informed. He was assured that the conclusions regarding censorship in European and African areas would,

21

according to the views of the State Department, also apply to Asia-Pacific areas.[5]

On May 19, 1944, a message was sent from the War Department to the commander-in-chief of the Southwest Pacific Area, Douglas MacArthur. This was the first directive dispatched concerning civil censorship in this area, although censorship had "been constantly under study and [had] now taken a fairly definite shape."[6]

The directive stated that civilian censorship in occupied areas was the responsibility of the Supreme Military Commander. It mapped out the basic organization for such censorship under military command and underlined that the War Department was responsible for integration with all censorship agencies and activities.[7] An appendix attached to the directive outlined the reasons for civilian censorship. It was said to be imperative in order to obtain information of value in prosecuting the war effort and gauging the state of public opinion and morale, to aid in carrying out the policies of the military or other governments in the area and the governments of the United Nations. Through censorship it would also be possible to obtain information on trade, finance, and other subjects that would aid in the war effort. Further reasons for introducing civilian censorship were to maintain security, protect lines of communication, detect subversive elements, prevent information from reaching the enemy, and discover attempts to violate any military order or regulation in the area. Censorship would be in force during three different phases: the battle period, the occupation, and the period in which an indigenous government was installed. With regard to the occupation period, there should be severe restrictions on freedom to communicate. The reason, as explained in the appendix, was to reduce censurable material to amounts that could be handled by personnel from the United States and other countries—in short, simply from a practical point of view. The means of communication that were to be censored included mail, telegrams, and telephone as well as film and photographs. One area that later became an extremely important undertaking in Japan—censorship of what we now call mass media (newspapers, radio, books)—was not even mentioned.[8]

This was the first finalized plan for censorship in an area that included Japan. In a letter to U.S. Office of Censorship Director Price, who again had asked how the plans for censorship were developing, the Joint Chiefs wrote that civil censorship in Japan would be the largest by far. They presupposed that military control, including censorship, would be required there for a considerable time after the defeat. A special study was being prepared about that problem, and Price was invited to contribute.[9]

Price's continuing interest in censorship planning for the Pacific was revealed in still more letters. It was he who first took up the question of censorship of the press and broadcasting. In a letter to Chief of Staff Admiral William Leahy on September 11, Price pointed out that there was no reference at all to this question in the directives that had been sent to MacArthur in May. He was also still worried about planning in general. Although he had been told that this was the responsibility of the War Department, he felt that there should be more coordination between different agencies, such as his own Office of Censorship and the State, War, and Navy departments. He suggested that they get together for a conference on censorship.[10] In reply, Price got the names of two persons in the War and Navy departments, who were authorized to discuss censorship questions.[11]

On November 12 the Joint Chiefs finally completed their draft of a directive regarding censorship of civilian communications in areas occupied by the United States. The first plan compiled for such censorship, this directive underlined that civilian censorship was indeed a military measure, for which the Supreme Commander was responsible. Although he could modify the censorship as he saw fit, he had to obtain prior approval from the Joint Chiefs of Staff in order to terminate censorship.[12] This meant that although the day-to-day decisions on censorship belonged to

MacArthur, and although the War Department led and coordinated the planning of censorship operations, it was the Joint Chiefs who decided whether there was to be any censorship. In an appendix, the details of censorship operations were laid out in a manner similar to the memo attached to MacArthur's directive from the War Department in May. One decisive addition had been made: to the list of communications to be controlled were added publicity media—newspapers, books, and so forth.[13]

As the American forces drew nearer to Japan, the directives regarding censorship became more detailed. In January 1945 the Joint Chiefs issued a Political Directive for Military Government in the Japanese Outlying Islands. In it the Supreme Commander was especially instructed to prohibit the dissemination of Japanese militaristic and ultranationalistic ideology and propaganda in any form.[14]

On April 20, 1945, the first Basic Plan for Civilian Censorship in Japan was sent to the War Department by Brigadier General Thorpe of the Intelligence Section, U.S. Army Forces in the Far East. This plan was similar to that of the Joint Chiefs of Staff from November 1944, with the added judgment that the censorship should be strict but would be "comprehensible to the Japanese who imposed similar controls in the Philippines and presumably in other occupied areas." The basis for censorship would be "to assist in the enforcement of the free and factual dissemination of news based upon United Nations standards." The restrictions that would be applied to civilian communications would be items concerning troop moves, criticism of Allies, politics, rumors, codes, and such information as might disturb public tranquility.

At first glance these might seem like reasonable requirements during the occupation of enemy territory. But a closer examination shows that the restrictions were so general as to cover anything that might be needed. A paragraph under the heading "Theory of Operation" shows that the American mood was far from lenient:

As previously stated in this plan, civil censorship in Japan will be severely restrictive. It is designed to draw a ring around the Japanese-controlled area which will reduce the possibility of communications getting out of that area during the first and second phases [the battle period and the period of occupation; see above] and, during the third phase [the period during which an indigenous government is installed; see above] will facilitate the gathering of intelligence.[15]

Through a decision by the Joint Chiefs of Staff on May 24, the commander-in-chief for the army forces in the Pacific (i.e., MacArthur) became formally responsible for making all plans for civil censorship in Japan.[16]

The Basic Plan was revised several times. The third version, called the Revised AFPAC Basic Plan for Civil Censorship, was approved on September 30, 1945. It became the actual basis for civilian censorship in Japan.[17]

At the same time the plans for censorship were being developed, American plans for the Occupation in general proceeded. As with censorship, general Occupation planning was conducted within different departments. From time to time they consulted with each other. Already in February 1942 the State Department had established an advisory committee on postwar foreign policy. Within this committee, Japan specialists of the department undertook extensive studies of many different problems that might arise after the war. They encountered little initial interference from the White House or the Joint Chiefs of Staff.[18] In light of this early and ambitious interest of the State Department for postwar planning, it is ironic that the position of the department in the actual Occupation was reduced to the office of a political adviser (POLAD), who often complained that he had no influence on the policies of the General Headquarters of the Supreme Commander.[19] But during the planning stage the State Department was consulted by the War and Navy departments and delivered copious reports. One of the recommendations made was that the military government naturally had to safeguard the security of the occupying forces, but that apart from measures that would be necessary to accomplish that purpose, it should not aim to be punitive in character or needlessly humiliate the Japanese people.[20]

By December 1944 the planning for what was called Military Government for Japan was being done by three departments: State, War, and Navy. Each had its special office taking care of these questions. For State it was the Office of Far Eastern Affairs; for War, the Civil Affairs Division; and for Navy, the Office of Military Government. The War and Navy departments also coordinated army and navy responsibilities in the Joint Civil Affairs Commission. The discussions and decisions of the three departments took place in the State-War-Navy Coordinating Committee (SWNCC) (and its Subcommittee for the Far East), which formulated policies and gave basic approval on questions, which were then sent on for approval by the president. SWNCC then communicated these decisions to the Joint Chiefs of Staff, who could comment on them before finally informing the Supreme Commander, General MacArthur.

All through the military planning for postsurrender Japan, the basic premise during the discussions on different levels was that Japan had to become democratic or, from another viewpoint, demilitarized. On June 11, 1945, SWNCC stated in a document that the basic objectives of the postsurrender military government in Japan included ''creation of conditions which will insure that Japan will not again become a menace to the peace and security of the world.''[21]

In the detailed planning there was also always a paragraph concerning freedom of speech and of the press. In a June 1945 report by the Joint Civil Affairs Committee to the Joint Chiefs of Staff, the Initial Post-Defeat Policy Relating to Japan was explained in detail. Among important tasks to be undertaken at an early stage was an end to the dissemination of ideas subversive to the purposes of the United Nations. Instead, the military government should spread information and knowledge of the ideals in which the United Nations believed.[22]

The Basic Initial Post-Surrender Directive, dated August 29,

1945, which became the basis for the whole occupation of Japan, stated that "The Japanese people shall be encouraged to develop a desire for individual liberties and respect for fundamental human rights, particularly the freedoms of religion, assembly, speech, and the press."[23] This was completely in accordance with the Potsdam Declaration, the July 1945 Allied statement on the aims for postwar Japan. In the Declaration, the Japanese government was told to remove all obstacles to the revival and strengthening of democracy and to establish freedom of speech, religion, and thought as well as respect for fundamental human rights.[24] Armed with these ideals and directives, the U.S. Occupation Forces led by MacArthur landed in Japan. MacArthur himself touched ground at the Japanese Atsugi air base against the advice of those who feared that Japanese fanatics might be lurking around every corner. Everything went well, however, and on August 30, he established himself at the legendary Grand Hotel by the Bund in Yokohama. More American troops landed at the Yokosuka naval base, not far from Yokohama.

The surrender of Japan had come suddenly. The plans for invasion were aborted; instead, attention turned to the immediate implementation of occupation plans. MacArthur took the lead personally by issuing directives called SCAPINs (Instructions from the Supreme Commander of the Allied Powers) to the Japanese government.

On September 10, the Freedom of Speech and Press Directive was published. Government control of the press was to end and freedom to ensue:

> The Supreme Commander for the Allied Powers has decreed that there shall be an absolute minimum of restrictions upon freedom of speech. Freedom of discussion of matters affecting the future of Japan is encouraged by the Allied Powers unless such discussion is harmful to the efforts of Japan to emerge from defeat as a new nation entitled to a place among the peace-loving nations of the world.[25]

On September 22, the Japanese government was told to disassociate itself completely from the press so that liberal tendencies would be further encouraged. All news agencies, both national and international, should have free access to the news sources of the world and to all communications facilities. The government was to remove all controls, both direct and indirect, from newspapers and news agencies.[26]

Three days later the Japanese government was once more told to relinquish its control of the media. This included repealing all laws through which censorship had been practiced, and prohibiting any pressure on the media to compel conformity with any editorial policy that was not its own. But a hint that freedom was incomplete, indeed, that possibly only the censorship masters had changed, appeared via the statement that only restrictions that were specifically approved by SCAP would be permitted in the censorship of the written and spoken word.[27]

The Japanese government for the most part followed the American directive, but there was at least one case in which it did not. This became evident when two American correspondents, Frank Kluckhohn of the *New York Times* and Hugh Baillie, president of United Press, on the same day each managed to get an interview with the emperor. The large Tokyo dailies *Asahi, Mainichi,* and *Yomiuri-Hochi* had managed to get hold of the interview and were preparing to publish it in their morning editions of September 29, when they were ordered by the Ministry of Home Affairs to suspend the issue. Along with the Cabinet Information Bureau, it was this ministry, with its Censorship Section of the Police Bureau, that transmitted American directives to all media. According to U.S. records of the incident, the five large Tokyo newspapers jointly entered an agreement with the Ministry of Home Affairs not to publish anything about the interview with the emperor. It seemed that at least the three of them regretted this decision, however, because they published the interview after all. In the same issue they published photos from the emperor's visit to MacArthur. According to the secretary of the Board of Information, the main objection was the story by Kluckhohn, because in it the emperor seemed to criticize General

Tojo by name, something the board believed "might lead to public disturbances." When the meddling of the Ministry of Home Affairs became known to SCAP, the newspapers were notified that they were indeed allowed to send out their papers, on the basis of the guidelines of September 29 that prohibited government pressure on the media. The government itself was notified through the ordinary channel for information between itself and SCAP, the Liaison Office.[28]

A few days later, October 4, the Japanese government was presented with the Civil Liberties Directive, which concerned the elimination of restrictions on political, civil, and religious rights. Freedom of speech and of the press were thereby proclaimed. From November 1, the powerful Board of Information was reorganized on SCAP orders. The board had effectively controlled the press through different means, including censorship. Its new assignment was to collect information regarding national policies and public opinion and to offer services to the press and radio, as well as assisting different cultural enterprises. The censorship section was abolished. But after two months, the Civil Information and Education Section of SCAP decided to abolish the board altogether on December 31, 1945.[29] The Japanese government had lost its powers to direct and restrict thoughts, speech, and writing. In the new constitution, which went into effect May 3, 1947, these rights were established. Article 21 said plainly: "No censorship shall be maintained, nor shall the secrecy of any means of communication be violated." The aim of the Allied Powers, as stated in the Potsdam Declaration, and of the United States, as stated in the Basic Initial Post-Surrender Directive, had been accomplished, executed by the Supreme Commander for the Allied Forces in the Pacific, General Douglas MacArthur.

In contrast to these well-publicized instructions declaring Japan a country with basic freedoms, including freedom of speech, the planning and practical work of the Civil Censorship Detachment, from the beginning of September, was as secret as all the discussions and plans for its implementation had been.

While conferring freedom with one hand, the United States severely controlled it with the other through its own censorship.

Censorship was not a totally foreign concept to the United States in spite of American popular emphasis on freedom. The Office of Censorship, which had been inaugurated at the beginning of the war against Japan, kept strict censorship on material entering and leaving the United States. By pointing to the war situation, it also saw to it that the American press kept within certain boundaries.

Regarding the extensive planning for censorship in a future occupied Japan, an interesting question is whether this censorship was instigated as a normal action of occupation forces to be taken during war in any territory that was conquered. The alternative was that from the outset it was accepted as a civilian, not a military, operation. The activities of the (civilian) director of the U.S. Office of Censorship in prodding the War, Navy, and State departments toward action in planning for censorship of occupied territories seem to show that he, Price himself, was at least as intent on controlling the future defeated enemies through censorship as the military was. In fact, one gets the impression that certain aspects of censorship planning—for example, the introduction of media censorship—would have taken much longer to come into being had it not been for Price's planting of such thoughts within the concerned departments.

Obviously, censorship to a certain extent is a normal military undertaking in occupied territories. What form it would have taken had Byron Price not acted is a moot point, because the fact is that he did act. Consequently, it can be said that the introduction of censorship in Japan was at least partially a civilian initiative.

It can also be said that the control of censorship in Japan ultimately was in civilian hands. Although the Supreme Commander had the responsibility to execute and modify censorship, he could not terminate it without prior approval by the Joint Chiefs of Staff, who were subject to the decisions of the president.[30]

A further question concerns the purpose of censorship. Although the stated purpose in the Basic Plan was to control the defeated country in order to accomplish occupation goals, the measures clearly clashed with the swift actions to demilitarize and democratize Japan. The fact that the democratization process was widely publicized whereas the existence of censorship was kept secret raises new questions.

SCAP TAKES CHARGE OF THE JAPANESE PRESS

THE POWER of General MacArthur, the Supreme Commander in Japan, was based on several documents. On September 6, 1945, he received one of them, instructions from the Joint Chiefs of Staff that, from now on, both the emperor and the Japanese government were to obey him. He was given a very free hand: "You will exercise your authority as you deem proper to carry out your mission." He was told that he had supreme power and did not need to explain any measures to the Japanese. He was also informed that he could enforce his orders in any way he liked, including the use of force.[1] In the Basic Initial Post-Surrender Directive, which was issued by the president and finally reached Japan in its definitive form on November 8, 1945, the details of his duties were spelled out, much as they had tentatively been presented in earlier directives. Among the many points was the question of civilian censorship. This should be established over mail, wireless, telephone, telegraph and cables, films, and the press "as may be necessary in the interests of military security and the accomplishment of the purposes set forth in this directive."[2]

The purposes set forth were basically the same as those in the Potsdam Declaration through which the Allies presented their demands on Japan for surrender. But the authorship of that document belonged to a U.S. State-War-Navy Subcommittee, which had prepared the document for President Truman to bring with him on his journey to Potsdam in July 1945.[3] It called on Japan to become a democratic country but did not contain any details about how this was to happen, apart from the obvious demand that the present Japanese government had to surrender.

The planning and organization of the practical aspects of the Occupation had started at the headquarters of the United States Army Forces in the Pacific under General MacArthur. A special government military section had had the responsibility of organizing the future military government in Japan. The assumption of this section was that the U.S. military government in Japan would be vast, just as it was in Germany and Italy. MacArthur, however, challenged this concept. He preferred a system whereby the Japanese government would continue to be responsible for the execution of policies that were set down by SCAP. SCAP would, so to speak, supervise the work of the Japanese government, assisted by his headquarters. As far as MacArthur was concerned, he might just as well transfer his existing headquarters from Manila to Tokyo.[4] This sounded simple but was an invitation to criticism. MacArthur's headquarters in Manila was the headquarters of the Commander-in-Chief of the U.S. Army Forces in the Pacific, whereas in Tokyo he would be Supreme Commander for the Allied Powers, responsible not only for American but also for Allied forces if they came to Japan. MacArthur managed to have his own plan accepted, and to a large extent he simply transferred his Manila headquarters to Tokyo, where it received its new name, SCAPHQ (most often simply called GHQ). In this way the organization of the Occupation headquarters was largely the same as that of a conventional military staff. Many of its leading officers were the same ones who had been with MacArthur in wartime.

The SCAP headquarters was organized into General Staff sections (see figure 1). As in war, the Intelligence Section was named G-2, and as had been the case during the war in the Pacific, its head was General Charles Willoughby.[5] He took on the work with enthusiasm: ''MacArthur's G-2 promptly oriented

Figure 1. **The Staff of SCAP**

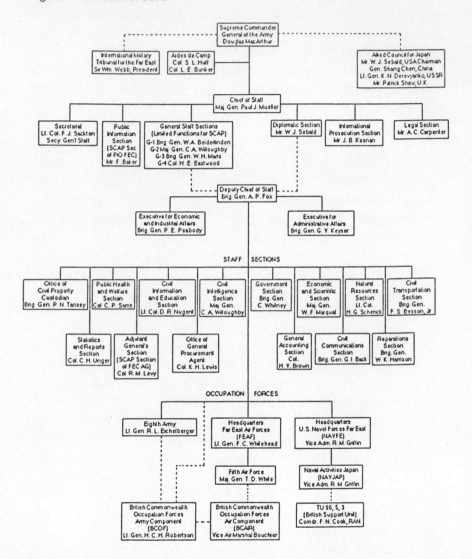

his wartime apparatus toward 'civil' rather than 'military' intelligence. A newly created 'Civil Intelligence Section' operated in fairly well-defined channels, and the old G-2 'workhorses' pulled in fresh harness."[6]

The Civil Intelligence Section (CIS), received almost all of its information on subversive activities in Japan from the Counter-Intelligence Corps, whose work was "roughly analogous to that of the American FBI."[7] It had many different departments, one of which was the Civil Censorship Detachment (CCD).[8] CCD in its turn was divided into bureaus, which handled different aspects of censorship (see figure 2). The one dealing with censorship of mass media was called the Press, Pictorial and Broadcast Division (PPB). It started its work the moment the Occupation officially got underway, that is, September 2. Censorship of the press in Tokyo was introduced that very day, although on a limited basis. With only a limited number of staff yet available, only the English-language *Nippon Times*, a mouthpiece of the Foreign Ministry, and the news agency Domei and similar news services were put under precensorship. The Japanese-language papers were put under postcensorship, which meant that they could publish what they saw fit, but that they did it at the risk of some form of later punishment, if their information violated the rules. What these rules were was not yet stated.

It would be natural to think that since only papers and news agencies in Tokyo were checked, this left much freedom for papers outside the capital. The Japanese press was highly centralized, however, since news was often forwarded from Domei and the large Tokyo papers to local papers in different parts of the country. This system had obviously worked to the benefit of the harsh Japanese censorship system. It now turned out to be very helpful for the Americans as well. It was important to control the Tokyo media, because then "a great part of the material disseminated to the Japanese people could be controlled at its source."[9] Indeed, the Americans had been planning to rely on the old Japanese censorship organization. "Wherever possible" the physical facilities of the Japanese censorship organization would be made "full use" of.[10]

The first guidelines for the Japanese press were sent to the government on September 10. SCAP said that the Japanese government must see to it that no false news was published. At the same time, there were limitations on truth: apart from information that would disturb public tranquility, it was prohibited to discuss unreleased Allied troop movements, to criticize the Allied Powers ("false or destructive"), and to spread rumors. Radio broadcasts came under particular scrutiny. They would, for the time being, only be allowed to contain news, music, and entertainment. Radio Tokyo would be the only station allowed to broadcast news, comments, and information. Any media violating the guidelines would be suspended.[11] The same day, CCD held a conference with officials of the Japanese government, who were told how censorship would work. It was established that in the future, at least for the time being, all contact between CCD and Japanese radio and press representatives would be conducted through the Board of Information.[12] The Censorship Section of the Police Bureau in the Ministry of Home Affairs and the Cabinet Information Bureau transmitted SCAP instructions to newspapers and other media.[13] Also, there was a system by which each paper in effect censored itself by appointing its own overseers. They checked articles in order to eliminate those that could be expected to be censored by the authorities. These overseers, or "self-censors," remained in the newspaper offices during the Occupation.[14] This system can hardly have convinced Japanese journalists that press freedom now reigned. They were in fact controlled through the very same institutions that had censored all their stories during the war.

Only a few days after the announcement on press freedom and its limitations, the first punishment was meted out. This was a complicated problem concerning the central news agency Domei. Domei not only disseminated news inside Japan; it also had overseas broadcasts, both plain and in Morse. Since its creation by the

37

Figure 2. Organization Chart of the Civil Censorship Detachment

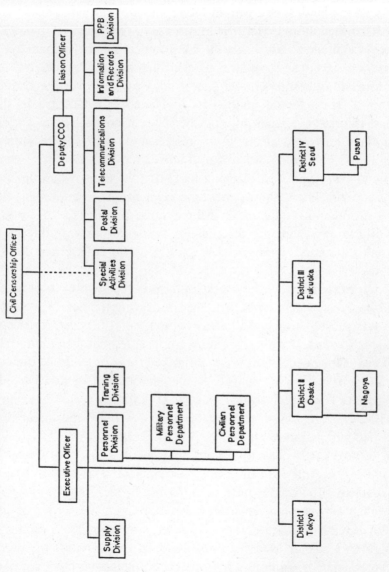

Source: SCAP, box 8524.

government in 1936 as a completely state-run agency, it had taken on different duties. When Nagasaki was bombed and the Soviet Union declared war on Japan, the government, in the general confusion and need for information, made use of Domei's lines from Nagasaki (where the communications from Manchuria and the new war front first reached Japan). A wide variety of information, both open and classified, was sent over the Domei lines.[15] Thus, Domei journalists in Nagasaki were perhaps the best informed Japanese during the days of confusion in August 1945. Domei was also able to broadcast abroad, if not at home, the news that Japan was about to surrender. This had been done already on August 10. Despite fears that the army would launch a coup if it knew about government intentions to surrender, the government used Domei's Morse code broadcasts to let the world know. Evidently the censors, who were serving the interests of the army, overlooked this more obscure dissemination of news.[16]

On September 10, however, SCAP ordered Domei to suspend all its overseas shortwave broadcasts. During the next three days it was closely watched by CCD, which led to further American dissatisfaction. As a consequence, on September 14 Domei had to cease for twenty-four hours all its overseas broadcasts, including those in Morse, as well as the distribution of news inside Japan. CCD complained of "coloration of local news."[17] In a PPB manual, Domei was accused of having spread news that disturbed public tranquility.[18]

What exactly was this news that seemed so threatening to SCAP? The American listening post Magic was tuned in to the Japanese broadcasts during this time. Under the heading of "Japanese exploitation of atomic bombing," the writer of the Magic report for September 13 quoted a message from Japanese Foreign Minister Mamoru Shigemitsu to the Japanese legations in Sweden, Switzerland, and Portugal emphasizing the wide coverage of the atomic bomb damage in Hiroshima and Nagasaki. He also mentioned an American investigation party that had gone to Hiroshima and Nagasaki, and the comments of the head of the group, Brigadier General Thomas F. Farrell, who reportedly said that the damage at Hiroshima was beyond description, and that so horrible a weapon must never be used again. The foreign minister went on to say that Domei had sent abroad in full detail all the reports he mentioned. The Magic writer added a note: "General MacArthur today issued an order restricting Domei to the distribution of news inside Japan."[19]

That news and information concerning the conditions at Hiroshima and Nagasaki was regarded as disturbing public tranquility would not be an isolated case; articles, books, and other items dealing with the results of the atomic bombings would be suppressed with the same motivation during the coming years.

The suspension of Domei was put into effect through the formal channel that had been decided upon a few days earlier—the Japanese Board of Information. But to make sure that the orders were obeyed, censorship officers were also stationed inside the Domei building. The president of Domei and other representatives of press and radio were summoned to CCD, where "orders were precisely and forcefully presented."[20] At a meeting called the next day, Japanese press people were told that the Supreme Commander was not satisfied with the manner in which they had carried out the directive. "Freedom of the press is very dear to the Supreme Commander, and it is one of the freedoms for which the Allies have fought," the Civil Censorship officer told them. He pointed out that Domei had been suspended for disseminating news that disturbed public tranquility and talked of "the tone of the colored news." This concerned the relations between the Occupation forces and the Japanese. The Japanese were accused of giving the impression that MacArthur was negotiating with the Japanese government, not on any particular question but in general. They were emphatically told that the Japanese public should not be permitted to get a false idea of the position of the Japanese government vis-à-vis the Allied Powers. Japan was not negotiating but receiving orders dictated by the Supreme Commander.

The Japanese must not believe that they already had regained the respect of the world, nor that they in any way had regained a status whereby they could negotiate with anyone. The Japanese press had slanted the news, giving the opposite impression, and that was to be stopped at once. They were upsetting public tranquility by not telling the truth, the officer exhorted. As a consequence, MacArthur had decided on more severe censorship. One hundred percent censorship of the press and the radio would be continued. No more false or misleading statements nor any misleading criticism of the Allies would be permitted. The Japanese government was told to take measures to see to it that this policy was carried out at once. If it did not do so, the Supreme Headquarters would.[21]

The meetings between CCD officers and the Japanese press became a regular affair. CCD used meetings to admonish but also to teach the Japanese what kind of press the Occupation authorities expected. Like the Japanese government before them, the Americans not only censored what they regarded as unsuitable, but also sought to influence what was written and published. Already in September the Japanese press was watched closely for topics that the Allies wanted to be discussed publicly, such as war guilt. At a meeting in October, CCD noted that the press had started to give more space to foreign news, and to discuss war crimes.[22]

In spite of the seriousness of the meeting with Domei, the news agency was allowed to resume dissemination of news within Japan after twenty-four hours. It was subjected to full censorship, which meant that everything had to be checked by censors, but it was functioning. Activities were only allowed to resume as a matter of expediency for the Occupation authorities, however. By having Domei spread news to the provinces they could not only control what went out but also ensure that desirable news indeed reached the people. So dependent were the local newspapers on material from Domei that the Americans feared the smaller papers would have to close down if Domei stopped providing them with news. In Domei the Occupation authorities saw an effective means to control news dissemination to the Japanese people.[23] In other words, Domei played the same part of centrally controlled news disseminator to the Occupation forces as it had to the Japanese wartime rulers. In the latter capacity it had also been authorized to broadcast to Japanese troops overseas, of course under full censorship control.[24] At the end of October 1945, Domei was "voluntarily liquidated."[25] Two successors were founded—Jiji Press and Kyodo—both of which were still in operation in 1990.

Domei was not the only organization subject to control. The giant *Asahi* in Tokyo was suspended on September 18 for violating the Press Code on the same day the code was issued.[26] The Press Code guidelines were formulated in ten points:

1. News must adhere strictly to the truth.
2. Nothing shall be printed which might, directly or by inference, disturb public tranquility.
3. There shall be no false or destructive criticism of the Allied Powers.
4. There shall be no destructive criticism of the Allied Forces of Occupation and nothing which might invite mistrust or resentment of these troops.
5. There shall be no mention or discussion of Allied troops movements unless such movements have been officially released.
6. News stories must be factually written and completely devoid of editorial opinion.
7. News stories shall not be colored to conform with any propaganda line.
8. Minor details of any news story must not be overemphasized to stress or develop any propaganda line.
9. No news story shall be distorted by the omission of pertinent facts or details.
10. In the makeup of the newspaper, no news story shall be given undue prominence for the purpose of establishing or developing any propaganda line.[27]

In addition to the Press Code, the Civil Censorship Detachment distributed instructions regarding the censorship procedure.

One of the points in these instructions states that there must be no mention of censorship in the publications; neither must there be any traces, such as blank spaces, dots, circles, or blacked-out portions, that would imply censorship deletions.[28] Even those who were censored should receive only the most cursory information. No detailed explanations should be given to anyone censored. A simple statement would be given, nothing more. A stated reason for this secretiveness was that it would take too much time to explain every deletion. General discussion of censorship with the censored would also be avoided. The reason was simply that the problem of censorship ''is extremely sensitive.''[29]

Another problem was what the foreign press would say. Various non-Japanese news agencies, newspapers, and publishers might want to sell their material in Japan. In the beginning of the Occupation, no foreign mass media material, be it articles or films, was allowed into Japan. But already in the fall of 1945 CCD started worrying about what it would do when it became necessary to allow such material to be introduced.[30] It soon clashed with foreign correspondents about their reporting too.

The censors soon took new action against the Japanese press. Another twenty-four hour suspension was ordered, this time of the English-language *Nippon Times*, which had published an editorial on the new foreign minister. In principle, nothing seemed wrong with the article itself; the suspension was for having published it without submitting it to censorship first. *Nippon Times* tried to excuse itself by referring to editorial oversight, but the censorship authorities were not convinced and labeled the paper's action direct disobedience.[31]

After some more incidents, the five big newspapers of Tokyo—*Asahi*, *Mainichi*, *Yomiuri-Hochi*, *Nippon sangyo*, and *Tokyo shimbun*—were placed under precensorship as a further strengthening of censorship. Now they had to withhold publishing anything until it had been brought to the censorship office, checked and approved, and brought back for printing.[32] Gradually the censorship operations also branched out to other parts of the country outside Tokyo. This took time, however. It was the end of October before the Press, Pictorial and Broadcast Section established itself in the other big city area, Osaka, and introduced precensorship of seven newspapers, two news agencies, and broadcasts there.[33] As more censorship stations were established, the responsibility of the Tokyo District was alleviated, so that in February 1946 radio broadcasting also was permitted in Osaka, Fukuoka, and Nagoya, instead of all emanating from Radio Tokyo.[34]

The censorship was also extended to cover more of the media. In October, precensorship of books was initiated in the Tokyo area. Although there were severe shortages of everything, including paper, thirteen publications were brought under censorship during the first month.[35] The publishing industry grew quickly. By spring 1946, in one thirty-day period, 4,985 newspapers, 1,268 magazines, and 1,169 books were submitted for censorship.[36] In January 1946 the motion picture industry was informed that no film could be shown without prior clearance by the censors. Furthermore, everyone who owned films had to make a report of them. In March the Home and Education Ministries reported that they had accounts of 8,450 films.[37] Not even *kamishibai* performances, simple "paper movies" shown by itinerant storytellers, were exempted from censorship. In March 1946 the Press, Pictorial and Broadcast Section called a meeting with *kamishibai* producers in Tokyo and told them that censorship also applied to *kamishibai*.[38]

Means of communication other than mass media were also gradually more or less severely controlled. In September the Civil Censorship Detachment had taken over the Japanese postal system. Mail sent and received inside Japan as well as international mail came under close scrutiny.[39] Censorship of private mail was intended to keep the Occupation authorities informed about the extent and trend of acceptance by the Japanese of democratic principles. Through mail censorship they also hoped to gather information about a wide range of subjects, such as underground elements, black marketing, and war criminals.[40]

In the summer of 1946 the Civil Censorship Detachment was a sizable outfit with a total strength of 8,734 persons. There were 90 officers, almost as many enlisted men, several hundred War Department civilians, but, above all, non-American civilians, among them Japanese and Korean nationals. They were the ones doing the day-to-day censoring at lower levels, and nearly the only ones who knew Japanese. They numbered 8,084.[41]

As a further means of controlling and monitoring information to and from Japanese, a special section for American propaganda was established, called the Civil Information and Education Section (CIE). This organ was to utilize Japanese press, radio, motion pictures, schools, churches, and organizations of every kind to "remake Japanese thinking, impress war guilt on the nation, and expedite the Four Freedoms."[42] As part of its wide-ranging activities, this section collected presurrender Japanese literature, which was said to contain military propaganda.[43] The American journalist Mark Gayn, who worked and traveled widely in Japan during the first years of the Occupation, accompanied soldiers on such collection tours: "In all parts of Japan, small groups of Americans were searching schools—for caches of arms, for airplane parts, for posters extolling the virtues of war, for books dealing with Allied barbarism and spiritual inferiority."[44] Among books prohibited were schoolbooks. The children either were told to black out parts deemed unsuitable or were left without schoolbooks until new ones could be written and printed. CIE also initiated American-style radio-theater series telling about Japanese atrocities during the war.

Through banning books, censorship, and supplying material to be printed and broadcast, the Occupation authorities aimed to control information. These policies were no different from those of any totalitarian state. They covered all means of communication and set up rules that were so general as to cover anything. Yet the authorities did not specify subjects prohibited, did not state the punishment for violations—although it was clear that there were such punishments—and prohibited all discussion about the existence of censorship itself.

These policies were introduced at the same time that Supreme Commander Douglas MacArthur, who was ultimately responsible for the censorship activities, was emphatically telling the Japanese people and Japanese journalists that freedom of the press and freedom of speech were very close to his heart and were freedoms for which the Allies had fought the war.

THE ALLIES AND THE OCCUPATION

THE PLANNING for the Occupation of Japan was a completely American undertaking. The Soviet Union did not even enter the war until August 9, 1945, when it broke its neutrality pact with Japan. China was preoccupied with managing its own affairs. The Commonwealth countries, to a considerable extent, had a common strategy outside of their own territories, but Asia was mainly Southeast Asia, location of occupied colonies and China. There was little British planning and no significant British effort to influence Japan's future after the war.[1] It was not until the end of May 1945 that Foreign Secretary Anthony Eden asked Prime Minister Winston Churchill to approve the start of planning for British participation in the Occupation.[2] During the following four months the Foreign Office made some studies, but Churchill was uninterested even in the basic question of whether Britain should participate in the Occupation.[3]

The writing of the Potsdam Declaration, the basic document for the surrender of Japan, was an American undertaking, although it was presented as the joint policy of the Allied Powers. Britain had little opportunity to comment on it, China was shown the text just before it was made public, and the Soviet Union, which had not yet entered the war against Japan, was not consulted at all.[4] Neither was there any in-depth discussion about the arrangements for control and occupation of Japan among the Allies at the Potsdam conference.[5]

This was completely in accord with American wishes. In addition, SWNCC had decided in June that it was "militarily desirable that we deny to any other nation control of the occupation of the main Japanese islands."[6] The military continued its planning during the summer of 1945 without consultations with the Allies. The planning included such questions as how to follow up on a Japanese response to the Potsdam Declaration, and how to carry out the Occupation.[7] When Japan surrendered, it was the U.S. State Department that drafted the response, approved by the U.S. president. Clearly, the United States intended that the Allied commander in charge of the Occupation be an American. President Truman explained the position of the United States in no uncertain terms: "We wanted Japan controlled by an American commander. . . . I was determined that the Japanese occupation should not follow in the footsteps of the German experience. I did not want divided control or separate zones."[8]

Such a policy, taken without discussion with the other Allies, led to some difficulties, particularly with the Soviet Union, which made an attempt to obtain influence in the planned Occupation. The United States had its answer to Japan ready when Soviet Foreign Minister Vyacheslav Molotov called in American Ambassador to Moscow Averell Harriman and his British colleague Clark Kerr to read them the Soviet answer to the Japanese, which Molotov intended to be the joint Allied answer. On the same occasion, he also took up the question of the supreme commander for the Occupation. Harriman answered that the United States was ready to listen to advice from its allies, but he made it clear that it would not accept any veto to its suggestions. Molotov then mentioned the possibility of two supreme commanders, which Harriman stated was "absolutely inadmissible."[9]

In the end, the American will prevailed. On August 18, 1945, the president approved a SWNCC memorandum stating that the Allies had the right and the responsibility to participate in the Occupation, but that the American government must be in charge of carrying out the Occupation policies as well as providing most of the army for the Occupation. There would be no Occupation zones. Occupation troops from countries other than the United States would be unified under an American command.[10]

For civilian matters, SWNCC momentarily contemplated a Far Eastern Advisory Council. According to the view of a British foreign officer, the American purpose in establishing such a council was "mainly to serve as a moral umbrella for the conduct of their own policy toward Japan."[11] In April 1945, SWNCC had decided that this idea would be officially presented to the Allies only if they requested some means of influence.[12]

The Allies did become worried lest they should have no formal possibility to take part in shaping policy for and administration of Japan. When the Occupation started in September 1945, there was no forum where they could voice their ideas or complaints. There were different suggestions to remedy the situation, but not until the Moscow conference of the Allied foreign ministers in December 1945 was it finally decided how. An Allied Council, consisting of four members (the United States, the Soviet Union, China, and the Commonwealth, representing the United Kingdom, Australia, New Zealand, and India), would meet once every fortnight in Tokyo to discuss questions of day-to-day activities of the Occupation. A Far Eastern Commission (FEC), consisting of representatives for each of the Allies, would meet regularly, but less often, in Washington to formulate policies for the Occupation. The role of the United States in the Occupation was stated as preparing directives based on the policies of the FEC. The role of SCAP was to implement these policies.[13]

Neither of these institutions came to have any substantial influence on the Occupation. The main reason for the weakness of FEC was that the large number of members of different persuasions made it impossible to come to any decisions quickly. An example of the ineffectiveness of FEC is the handling of the Basic Post-Surrender Policy for Japan. This, the one basic document for Occupation policy, was transmitted to SCAP in September 1945, but it was not approved by FEC until June 19, 1947. By then its adoption or nonadoption had become a moot point as the Occupation was well entrenched. The final opposition to the document after nineteen months of wrangling came from the Australian delegate. Not surprisingly, he regarded it as "overtaken by events." In the end it was unanimously adopted.[14]

FEC's lack of influence was not altogether a result of Allied bickering. The Department of State stated clearly in a formulation of policy in 1946 that SCAP took many actions on his own initiative in order to implement broad directives issued by the U.S. government. If FEC considered reversing any policy, it should realize that this was politically undesirable in Japan. This standpoint was explained to the American representative on FEC. He was also made to understand that he should not discuss it in FEC meetings.[15] From an American point of view, there was no question about what "fundamental" powers SCAP had, and that they included the power to make policy decisions.[16]

In the Allied Council, the results were hardly better from the Allied point of view. MacArthur's chief of intelligence, Charles Willoughby, wrote that "it functioned mainly as a 'talk shop.' "[17] MacArthur himself attended only the opening session, where he told the members that the council would be exclusively consultative and advisory.[18] The Commonwealth representative, MacMahon Ball, called it "a failure, and at times a fiasco":

> At its inception, General MacArthur's representative treated it with frivolous derision. General MacArthur omitted to consult it on many major questions. The procedure prescribed for providing members with information severely limited their opportunities to give informed advice. The representatives to SCAP showed exceptional sensitiveness to any question or comment which might be construed as criticism of any aspect of the Occupation.[19]

In an interview with the American journalist Mark Gayn, Ball said: "Our difficulty does not lie in a scarcity of experts. It lies in the fact that it's simply useless to bring any factual information before the Council, for it's immediately pounced on as an affront to the Supreme Commander.''[20]

But the lack of Allied influence was not solely the result of MacArthur's personal ambitions. As the world situation changed, so did the relationship between the former Allies. In 1948 the State Department in top secret recommendations cited ''the serious international situation created by the Soviet Union's aggressive Communist expansion.'' It called for no change in control of Japan and barred a peace treaty, and also encouraged MacArthur to make greater use of his authority to establish firm U.S. positions.[21]

Under these circumstances, the U.S. allies might harbor doubts about the Occupation and also voice them in FEC and the Allied Council, but they could not expect any results if these doubts concerned such basic questions as the reversal of policies in the economic and political fields, which took place from 1947. Japan was being openly groomed to become an ally of the United States.

If it was difficult for Commonwealth countries to influence the course of the Occupation, it was even more so for the Soviet Union. In May 1945 the Joint Chiefs of Staff had decided that Soviet entry into the war against Japan was no longer necessary. But at Yalta the promise had been made that the Soviet Union would enter the war against Japan within three months after the surrender of Germany, and so it did. Once Japan had surrendered, however, the Soviet Union was more interested in Manchuria, northern Korea, Sakhalin, and the smaller islands north of Hokkaido than in Japan proper. Although the Soviets suggested that they should occupy the northernmost large Japanese island of Hokkaido, they did not pursue the idea with any fervor, and it was, of course, at once rejected by the Americans.

This did not mean that the Soviet Union was completely uninterested in the Occupation. As many as four hundred Soviet officials at a time joined government representative Lieutenant General Kuzma Derevyanko in Tokyo. In the Allied Council meetings, Derevyanko put forward many questions regarding the

Occupation. The few times censorship was discussed, it was often at his initiative. The reasoning was somewhat surprising. The censorship question became an example of the lack of real democracy being fostered by the Americans. But in the view of the Soviets, this was not because of the existence of censorship, but the opposite: censorship was not harsh enough.

Stalin himself had brought up the problem in the fall of 1945, when he met the American ambassador to Moscow Averell Harriman. Stalin complained that he could not understand why the Japanese press and radio were permitted to denounce the Soviet Union, which was an ally of the United States. "Was Japan a conquered country or not? Did any censorship exist there?" the memo from the meeting recalled Stalin as asking. According to Stalin, the Soviet representative in Japan had approached MacArthur about the problem. For a while the press attacks had subsided, only to be resumed again. "The Soviet Government would never permit such a thing to go on in its zones of occupation. If any newspaper in Rumania, for example, should attack the United States, its editors would be immediately punished," Stalin had explained.[22] Harriman answered that MacArthur was only carrying out policies that the Soviet government had agreed on.[23]

The United States was loath to listen to Soviet complaints. A memo from the first secretary at the U.S. Embassy in Moscow explained that Soviet criticism of the Occupation, "utilizing the Far Eastern Commission and the Allied Council," was done in the hope of discrediting SCAP and "provoking" international and domestic American interference.[24] The U.S. political adviser at GHQ in Tokyo (POLAD, the State Department representative) also distrusted the Soviet Union. He accused the Soviets of misusing the Allied Council, of striving to foster dissent and discontent among Japanese, and of furthering Communist propaganda. Generally speaking, they did "not wish the occupation to achieve the announced end agreed upon." Derevyanko had "endeavored to utilize the Allied Council as an inquisitorial and investigative body by presenting requests for unnecessarily detailed information on a wide range of subjects'' and demanded ''oppressive action against Japanese.''[25]

Derevyanko continued to take up complaints of the kind Stalin had voiced to Harriman. Two years after Stalin's concerns about censorship, Derevyanko stated in the Allied Council that the Japanese press carried propaganda hostile to the Soviet Union, especially regarding the gradual repatriation of the hundreds of thousands of Japanese soldiers kept in Soviet prison camps in Siberia after the surrender. The living conditions in such camps were horrendous, and as the soldiers started to come home, the facts slowly became known for the first time. That these ''fantastic stories'' could be published in Japan was the result of ''actions of American censorship in Japan,'' Derevyanko charged. The U.S. answer in the Allied Council was one of categorical denial. In September 1948, censors in Japan were finally expressly told that criticism of the Soviet Union was allowed.[26]

Some of the few real discussions on censorship in the Allied Council were brought up by Derevyenko. In July 1946 he demanded confiscation and pulping of fascist, ultranationalist, and anti-Allied literature, as well as punishment of those who hid such literature. He wanted special care to be taken so that valuable paper and manpower would not be wasted producing such material. The American representative answered guardedly that Japanese thinking must not be restricted. The Commonwealth representative warned that ''freedom must not suppress freedom.'' In conclusion, the American representative was of the opinion that there really was no problem, because there was constant surveillance. But the meeting broke up in what was close to a quarrel.[27] When the Soviet Union insisted on taking up the same question in August, the American representative reported to the State Department that he had categorically refused any ''book-burning campaign.'' ''To employ Nazi-like methods of suppression . . . would be to vitiate those rights [of thought and speech] and to sacrifice a matter of principle for no very great practical gain.'' To the Soviet Union, this was a ''pseudo-democratic stand . . . as far from democracy as heaven is from earth.'' In Austria, the Soviet representative said, the Allied Council had accepted similar Soviet suggestions. Surely ''American principles on this question in Europe are [not] different from those in Japan,'' the Soviet representative supposed.[28] SCAP, however, did not act on the Soviet protests.

The other Allies did not voice any substantial concern about censorship in the FEC or Allied Council. The exception concerned publication of Japanese technical reports about the atomic bombings of Hiroshima and Nagasaki. On this question the Allies, particularly the British, were more strict than the United States and supported a continued ban on publication. The United States, on the other hand, wanted to lift censorship in this area for its own reasons, among which were continued cooperation with Japanese scientists. For some time the British strictness prevailed.[29]

In the planning stages of censorship operations, the United States had been ready to cooperate with Great Britain. In a report submitted by Censorship Office Director Byron Price to President Truman on November 15, 1945, Price told of negotiations regarding censorship planning for Japan that he had begun with the British Imperial Censorship Office and the Canadian Censorship Office. Price suggested that ''a universal communications blockade'' should be imposed against Japan. The secretary of state explored the possibilities, but, judging from the replies from ''some nations,'' there was ''no hope for the plan's success.''[30]

Among the many Occupation questions the Allies concerned themselves with, censorship played a minor part. It was not on the urgent list, and it was never discussed in principle by either the Far Eastern Commission or the Allied Council. Censorship in itself seems to have been accepted as a matter of course. It was discussed only in the context of controlling and punishing the Japanese, specifically to control criticism and to limit their research. Whether censorship was contrary to their right of free speech and democracy seems never to have been seriously raised.

6

CENSORSHIP IN PRACTICE

AFTER the war, the husband of the poet Sadako Kurihara was the editor of a newspaper in Hiroshima. From the Occupation authorities he had received instructions explaining in English about "Censorship Requirements of Newspaper and Magazines—Precensorship of First Issue." Any text that he wanted to publish must first be set up in type, printed in two copies, and taken to the censor. After being censored, one copy would be returned to him with a stamp, either approved by the censor or with parts deleted. Not until he received the copy could he start printing. If something was to be deleted, it should be done in such a way that the deletions would be invisible.[1]

For Mr. Kurihara, and for every other publisher, censorship was not only a question of thoughts and words; it also meant wasted work involved in setting up an article or a whole book for printing. Censorship meant that there was always the risk of being presented with so many deletions, that the whole typesetting process would have to be done anew or be canceled totally. The number of articles and books that were never set up at all for fear of rejection is incalculable.

What happened to Mr. Kurihara's articles when he brought them to the censor? Because he lived in Hiroshima, he had to take them to the local Press, Pictorial and Broadcast section in Fukuoka. For censorship purposes, Japan had been divided into three districts (the fourth being the former Japanese colony of

54

Korea). District I covered Tokyo, Yokohama, and the parts north thereof, including Hokkaido. District II was the area around Nagoya, Osaka, and Matsuyama, on the main island of Honshu and Shikoku. District III covered the western and southern parts of Japan, including Hiroshima and Fukuoka, and Kumamoto on Kyushu (see figure 3).[2]

When Mr. Kurihara delivered his article for censoring to the District III office in Fukuoka, it entered "the flow of news copy." If the article contained controversial statements, it would have to go through all thirty-one prescribed steps before a final decision was made on whether it could be published (see figure 4). How long that took varied widely. The first person who touched it, the timer, also numbered, dated, and time-stamped the two copies before passing them on to the comment editor.

Every item was to be commented on. In the case of "unobjectionable material," only eight steps had to be passed. "Possibly objectionable material," on the other hand, was scrutinized by a news copy receiver and a senior news copy reviewer. If they thought that the material was objectionable, they gave it to the news copy censor. If he was of the same opinion, he asked for a translation. This was then given to the assistant chief, who could delete parts or suppress the whole. What was deleted or suppressed had to be checked by the chief, and records were to be filed on the matter.

In the case of questionable items, the submitted material could be held until it was checked with other agencies. (This often happened with material about Hiroshima and Nagasaki). Generally sensitive items on which the chief did not want to take action himself were forwarded to the district PPB censor. He, in turn, could send the material to the central PPB Division, which could then delete or suppress.[3]

As a rule of thumb, all material could be divided into four categories: objectionable, questionable or possibly objectionable, sensitive, or unobjectionable. "Objectionable" was material that violated one or more articles of the Press Code or was considered

Figure 3. Area of Responsibility of Censorship Districts

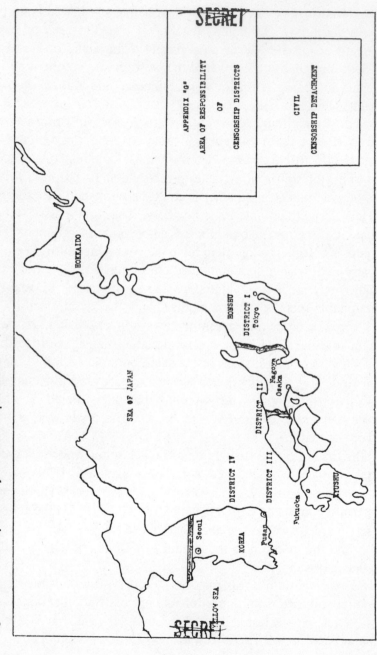

Source: SCAP, box 8524.

Figure 4. Organization of News Agency Department, PPB, CCD

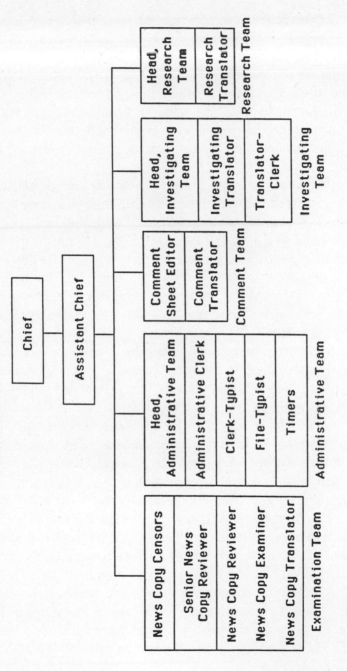

Source: SCAP, box 8569.

undesirable according to current censorship policies. "Questionable" material depended on the circumstances and was to be referred to the next higher authority before passing. "Sensitive" material should be referred to the district PPB censor. This included articles on General MacArthur, citizens of Allied countries in Japan, exports and imports, Occupation policies, and subjects included in key logs (see below) and other instructions. "Unobjectionable" material, of course, did not violate the Press Code.[4]

According to the instructions, if an article was partly deleted or completely suppressed, the newspaper or news agency submitting it should be informed immediately by telephone. If an item was referred to the district PPB censor, the reason for the delay was to be reported. Responsible for the overall censorship policy of the subsection was the chief for that subsection. But he had to maintain liaison with his immediate superiors in the PPB as well as with other subsections, and also with the precensored newspapers in his area.[5]

Such an elaborate censorship organization clearly demanded numerous personnel. In the early stages of planning censorship operations in Japan, the organizers were astounded at how difficult it was to find persons who knew Japanese.[6] Even before the war between Japan and the United States broke out, military organs concerned with intelligence gathering had warned of the lack of Japanese-speaking personnel. During the war, the navy in particular undertook to educate personnel in translating and interpreting. The program was very effective, and some of the pupils became the foremost U.S. specialists on Japan after the war. But their numbers were hopelessly inadequate. Therefore, it was decided to use nisei—Americans of Japanese parentage. (That nisei would come to be regarded as indispensable during the Occupation of Japan was ironic, since so many Japanese-Americans spent the war gathered in camps, considered enemy aliens.) But according to some accounts, as is the case with many second generation immigrants, the nisei knew surprisingly little of their parents' language. In one special test, only 3 percent were found to be fluent, and another 4 percent proficient. Thus, the nisei had to attend Japanese language training school, and neither they nor the other American students knew very much about Japan. The total number of American personnel schooled in Japanese language during the war did not rise much over a few thousand. Only a small portion of them would be involved with the Occupation of Japan for any extended period, and even fewer with the censorship operations.[7]

The requirements for censors were very demanding. A censor with the Newspaper Department must not only be thoroughly familiar with censorship regulations in general, but also should be able to handle administrative duties, interview publishers, undertake investigations, and observe trends in newspapers that were submitted for censorship (see figure 5).[8] The censor was supposed to have a comprehensive knowledge of both written and oral Japanese in addition to "excellent" knowledge of English, "preserving in all translations the exact shade of meaning of the original Japanese text." Finally, he must know the terms applicable to different activities of the Occupation as well as to world affairs.[9]

In light of the language requirements, it is not surprising that the majority of the censorship personnel were not Americans. In May 1946 the total staff of the Civil Censorship Detachment, covering all forms of censorship, comprised 8,734 persons. Of these, 8,084 were listed as foreign—Japanese and Korean nationals.[10] Most, if not all, it must be supposed, were found in Japan. They included Japanese with one non-Japanese parent, who had suffered during the nationalistic period of the 1930s and 1940s for being only half-Japanese and were now ready, even eager, to work for the Americans. There were also a number of foreign nationals who had lived out the war in Japan, often under difficult circumstances. Many Koreans, regarded in Japan as less than human, had been forced into hard labor there and did not mind working for the Americans. Even many Japanese who had a

Figure 5. **Flow of Newspaper Material Being Censored**

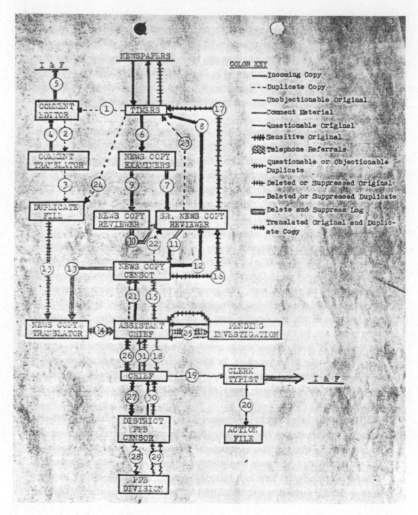

Source: Civil Censorship Department District II, PPB Section, News Agency Sub-section, Standard Operating Procedure and Distribution of Work, May 1, 1947, SCAP, box 8576.

knowledge of English were employed by the Americans in different positions, some of them as lower-echelon censors. They did not think of themselves as collaborators. They were enthusiastic young men and women who had kept up their interest in English in spite of all difficulties during the war. Now their language knowledge gave them a rare chance to find work when so many others were hungry and jobless.

Special censorship schooling was arranged for the non-American censors. The six-hour courses were designed to teach the basics of press censorship but also to "raise moral of Japanese Nationals by putting emphasis on their contribution towards the reconstruction of a free Japan." In a "slow, simple manner . . . due to the limited English potential of many of the students," they heard lectures on "The Press in the United States," "Mechanics of Press Censorship," "News Slanting," and "Divide and Conquer."[11]

The censorship department was plagued by too much work. Sometimes censorship demanded too many complicated decisions. In October 1946, PPB District I was reorganized as well as enlarged. One reason was "the growing sensitivity of press censorship," which required more efficient operation of the News Agency Section.[12] Another reason was the development of the media. When Japan surrendered, paper was in extremely short supply and was allocated centrally, but gradually the situation eased. According to the undetailed, rudimentary statistics made by CCD at the time, in 1945 the average number of newspapers censored monthly was 621; in 1947, 8,626. There were 99 books censored in 1945 and 1,660 in 1947. The ratios were similar for magazines.[13] No complete tabulations on type of censorship (total suppression, pages, lines, or words deleted) have been found by this writer.

The rules under which the censors worked were laid down in different manuals, subject matter files, and key logs. The manuals were handbooks for practical work and included the basic philosophy of censorship. The subject matter files were compilations of items that were of interest to different departments. Key logs included instructions on action to be taken when specific information was encountered. They were frequently changed and added to—for instance, in case of threatening strikes. For a certain period, strikes became taboo in the news through a special key log.[14]

In the PPB *Manual on Censorship in Japan* issued in September 1945, the censors were told that their primary mission was to insure that the efforts of Japan to emerge from its defeat as a new nation, entitled to a place among the peace-loving nations of the world, would not be harmed. Harm would be done, however, if anything was published that disturbed public tranquility and the welfare of Japan. A second mission of the censors, they were told, was to obtain information that would help to insure compliance with the terms of surrender.[15] What exactly would disturb public tranquility was not strictly defined.

> While "information that disturbs public tranquility" is a vague definition, it nevertheless is one which will enable suppression of any publication or radio station violating censorship and at the same time it carries a connotation of primary interest in Japanese welfare.[16]

Such concern about the welfare of Japan might enable American newspaper publishers who otherwise advocated freedom of the press to approve of censorship in Japan and, in turn, to shift American public opinion in favor of it.[17] In the beginning of the Occupation, the authorities were anxious to explain censorship to foreign correspondents and eager to foster the image that it somehow was a democratic undertaking. Counter-Intelligence Chief General Elliott Thorpe, who was responsible for the Civil Censorship Detachment, planned a special press conference on censorship for foreign correspondents because he realized that it was an extremely sensitive question. He made clear to the correspondents that the press conference was a unique occasion. He wrote in a memorandum that afterward censorship would no longer be discussed so openly. He took pains to underline that actually nothing would be censored unless it was untrue or "disturbed public tranquility." He then went on to explain what would be objectionable: no criticism of General MacArthur's Occupation policy would be allowed, whether it originated in the United States or elsewhere, if it was deemed "sufficiently serious" to upset public tranquility. An Allied power could criticize another Allied power. China could be criticized, both by others and by Chinese Communists. Quoting people under the sovereignty of a foreign power, even if they were critical, was also allowed. In addition, one might print discussions on the relations between the United States and the Soviet Union "provided their stated source is authentic." The Japanese could, indeed, both originate and print criticism about any world problem that did not "hamper" the Occupation aims, although the criticism must not, of course, be destructive. Thus, according to General Thorpe, they were allowed to write about President Truman's policies in the United States, about what a journalist personally thought would be the solution to the atomic bomb question, and about Allied policies in occupied Germany.[18] As an explanation of subjects permitted and not permitted in the Japanese press, however, Thorpe's memorandum was far from complete.

The prohibited subjects could be enumerated in much greater detail for practical purposes. A Monthly Operation Report from the PPB in November 1946 includes a guide to deletions and suppressions made during the time covered by the report. It has a whole list of key words with explanations. Besides criticism of SCAP ("any general criticism of SCAP and criticism of any SCAP agency not specifically listed below"), the United States, and the Allies, it also included "Criticism of Japanese Treatment in Manchuria," "Criticism of Allies Prewar Policies," "Third World War Comments," "Militaristic Propaganda," and "Justification or Defense of War Criminals." "Other Propaganda" was a heading that could be used for any propaganda not specifically listed. Not only was "Criticism of the Occupation Forces" not allowed, neither were stories on "Fraternization." "Black Market Activities" could not be mentioned, and "Overplaying Starvation" was prohibited. There was also a heading called "Premature Disclosure" and, of course, "Reference to Censorship."[19]

The interest of the censorship authorities did not stop at those subjects. Censorship was, after all, not only a question of limiting the output of information. Another important function was to gather intelligence. This was done through a thorough reading of material for publication or, later, when postcensorship became dominant, of already published material. It was also accomplished through the extensive mail, telephone, and telegraph censorship that began with the arrival of the first advance echelons of the Censorship Detachment in September 1945. For these censorship activities there were subject matter guides. In January 1946 such a guide was distributed to all the U.S. forces engaged in occupation of different areas of the world, including Japan. It had been compiled by the War Department according to the wishes of different agencies within the War, Navy, State, Treasury, and Justice departments. These agencies were expecting reports in the form of submission slips or comment sheets on the subjects listed, to be supplemented as required by the situation.[20]

The Subject Matter Guide itself was a six-page list of key words with short explanations of a few lines. It ranged from civil affairs and climate to espionage, finance, food, and narcotics. It mentioned politics, religion, terrain, and topography. The last subject on the list was war criminals, under which was specified any apparent serious mistreatment of U.S. personnel while prisoners of the enemy, identification of officer guards in German- or Japanese-controlled POW camps, and information on atrocities.[21]

In a separate Examiner's Requirement Guide, issued by the Office of the Chief of Counter-Intelligence of the United States Army Forces in the Pacific, subjects of special interest in Japan were listed. The key words included some in the more general guide, but some subjects were more detailed or included areas not mentioned in connection with the other occupied areas, such as information about new weapons, including atomic research, and even art treasures. Information about chemical warfare was another subject that evidently was pursued with intense interest.[22] "Escapes and escapees," concerning escape routes taken by POWs, were to be classified "Secret." Facts about the government and its personalities, reports of negotiations with other countries, policies of political groups, the Imperial Household Ministry, health (state of health of armed forces or civilian population), industry (production, development, expansion, etc.), and labor (present conditions, organization before, during, and after the war) were all regarded as valuable.[23]

In a special Subject Matter Guide for the Press, Pictorial and Broadcast Division there was also a list of persons about whom information was wanted in case it was spotted in any connection. The list mainly included persons believed to be liberal, or at least untainted by militarism.[24] They were regarded as suitable for leadership positions in the new, postwar Japan, or perhaps otherwise suitable for the Americans to cultivate. In other words, all information not only on the present state of the country but also on the basic organization of Japanese society was important.[25]

The key logs, which could be in force for a long or short time and were sometimes recalled and reissued, contained explicit directions on deletion of specific subjects. On January 2, 1948, a new key log supplement went into force with the direction that all previous key logs not only were rescinded but should be collected and burned. The key logs were treated as important documents over which rigid surveillance should be kept.[26]

At that late date, the key log still contained a score of forbidden subjects, including several that were familiar from the early Occupation—for instance, "Resentment of Allied Forces." One way such resentment was expressed would be by depicting the mode of living of the Allied forces as luxurious compared to that of the Japanese. Any reference to censorship was still prohibited.

Figure 6. **An Example of Censorship: Article by Saburo Okita, "Japan Views Her Reparations,"** *Contemporary Japan* **(January–March 1947)**

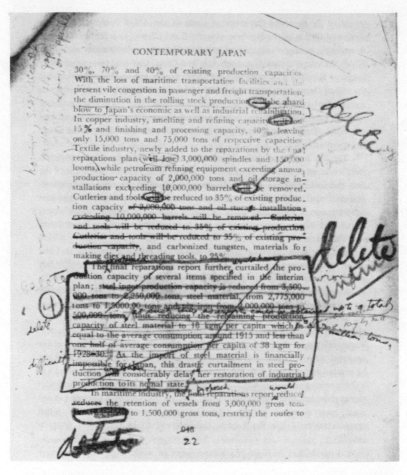

Source: The Gordon W. Prange Collection, The East Asia Collection, McKelden Library, University of Maryland.

So was any reference to particular sections within the SCAP. One could not write about Emperor Hirohito as a ruler, and one might not call for the end of the Occupation or for a peace treaty. As a new addition, it was forbidden to comment on or refer to Eniwetok, where the United States tested atomic bombs. In general, results of atomic tests were not to be published.[27]

The key logs occasionally were added to in view of some current topic. In April 1946, when the first Japanese cabinet was being selected as a result of the first elections after the war, guidelines were issued to the censors on how to deal with that subject in print. The elections had been presented as the first free elections in Japan; new parties were formed, radical politicians let out of jail, and women allowed to vote for the first time ever. The problem with the elections (as well as with the new constitution) was that too many people thought they were the work of SCAP, not of the Japanese government. Accounts from the time and research have shown that this was indeed correct,[28] but during Occupation, with the help of censorship, the fiction was upheld in the press. Judging from the key logs, SCAP wanted to be seen solely as giving advice; all decisions, including the selection of a new cabinet, were to be seen as made freely and independently by the Japanese themselves. According to the key log addition, general statements to the effect that MacArthur maintained a "hands-off" policy regarding the cabinet were to be passed. Vague references implying that one or more cabinets had been submitted for approval were to be deleted. A "Hold" (meaning that the item could not be printed but was not definitely suppressed; a decision would come later) was to be stamped on stories that maintained that a list of cabinet members had been submitted. Finally, any story claiming that the new cabinet must have approval from the United States government and the Allied representatives of the Far Eastern Council was to be completely suppressed.[29]

With guidelines such as these, the censors went to work. They had an almost endless number of cases to decide upon every day.

Figure 7. **Censorship of Foreign-Produced Material**

Source: The Gordon W. Prange Collection, The East Asia Collection, McKelden Library, University of Maryland.

During different periods and depending on different media, pre- or postcensorship was in force. Even the emperor was censored: the imperial rescript promulgating the new constitution was pre-censored—and passed—on November 3, 1946.[30] Subjects concerning the emperor were often suppressed. One example is a book called *Democracy and the Japanese Constitution,* which could not be published because, as the censor commented, it was a typical example of the definition of the emperor as divine and of the Japanese super-race theory.[31] For the same reason there were several complaints against a primer for English study which included phrases such as "according to the will of the Great Emperor Meiji." The sentence "Wherever they went, they carried with them the traditions, the habits, the ideas of the Mother Country" was deleted as "nationalistic propaganda."[32] "As the cherry is chief of flowers, so is the samurai chief of men" was regarded as glorification of feudal ideas, whereas "you have made a lieutenant of me but I will make a man of you" was militaristic propaganda.[33]

Also deleted were these lines from the book *Winter at a Sanatorium*: "On a fine day she took curtains and carpets out in the sun and beat them with a stick humming 'Damn Churchill, Damn Chamberlain.' Those were the days when Hitler was in the height of his reign and Maria was his ardent admirer."[34]

The question of the relationship between the Japanese and the Allied forces was sensitive. How sensitive the censors judged it to be can be surmised from the deletions they made. One poem was suppressed for containing criticism of the Allied powers and specifically the United States in the lines "Alas! What shall I do with those who come to me with their skin terribly burnt!" and "The sun is shining as in bygone days upon the streets that have turned into a scorched field wide and broad."[35] A love story could also contain sentences too delicate in that respect. For instance, "After she [a Japanese young woman called Tamiko] came to know Kent she began to take an interest in her friends' associations with their American boyfriends. Some were happy, some were miserable. She saw some tragedies too. But she always believed that she herself would never be placed in such a miserable plight. She often saw her friends fall in love with American soldiers. And she knew of cases where American soldiers left for home leaving heart-broken girls behind.'' The censor worried that this passage, written by an American correspondent, might arouse resentment of American Occupation forces.[36] He also thought that Japanese reading about Tamiko's visit to the Press Club might resent the standard of living of the Occupation forces in a nation on a subsistence diet, for ''when Tamiko sat at the table she felt very self-conscious. She knew that the Japanese waitresses were looking at her with great interest. . . . Fruit cocktails, bread and butter, tomato soup—the main dish was beefsteak, potatoes, peas and carrots. She could not believe her eyes when ice cream was served for dessert.''[37]

An example of how the provision concerning public tranquility was used is an article in *Hiroshima shimbun* in the summer of 1946. The headline read, ''They Slew or Sold Their Beloved Children. Dreadfully Piteous Condition of the Japanese in Manchuria.'' By 1946 Japanese who had emigrated to Manchuria in the 1930s gradually returned to Japan. Most were poor farmers or fishermen who had emigrated to the newly acquired Japanese colony in the hope of a better future. The government had encouraged, even forced, them to go there, promising land in abundance. But the emigrants often found that the land was far from civilization, and the closest contact with the rest of the world was a distant railway station. Through extreme difficulties they tried to eke out a living. They received no help from the Japanese Army, which at the time was fighting the Chinese in Manchuria. On the contrary, the men were drafted as soldiers, leaving the women and children to take care of the farming households, alone and unprotected. When the Soviet Union declared war on August 9, 1945, the settlers were panic-stricken, having been brought up on stories about the cruelty of Communists. The Japanese Army retreated, leaving the desperate civilians to their own means. The article in *Hiroshima shimbun* was an interview with a returnee from Manchuria, Hiroshi Hatamoto. He told how everybody had rushed toward the railway, hoping to catch a freight train going to the coast. The confusion was total, with many being trampled and run over by the train. The alternative to the train was a walk for thirty or forty days in burning sunshine during daytime and freezing cold at night through swamplands that could swallow a horse. Marchers, with enough food for only a few days, were attacked by bandits and ravaged by illness. Losing hope, mothers sold their children to local farmers: cheaper for those under five years of age, double price for those above. Others threw them into the river when they did not find anybody willing to buy the children rather than wait for them to die. Whole families committed suicide. Mr. Hatamoto's group lost 70 percent of its members. When they finally reached the coast, they were told of Japan's defeat. "No tears would come; no voice issued." But this was not the end of their ordeal. The Japanese in China had long been hated for the cruelty of their army. Now the two million immigrants, stranded in Manchuria, had to make a living. Many turned to robbery and prostitution in organized bands that marched forward like armies. Others, especially women, feared for their lives so much that they burnt and disfigured their faces with silver nitrate so that nobody would dare touch them.[38] The article was disapproved on grounds of violating paragraph 2 of the Press Code: "Nothing should be printed which might, directly or indirectly, disturb public tranquility."[39]

Articles or passages in books that showed that censorship existed were also banned. This happened with a book by Takashi Nagai, a Nagasaki doctor who had many difficulties with the censorship authorities because of his writings about the atomic bomb. "A farewell party was held at Tsutenkaku of [blacked out] five days before graduation" or "Ryukichi was called to the colors in the first mobilization of the [blacked out] Incident" did not pass, ostensibly because the blacked out portions were references to censorship.[40]

Some censors also saw themselves in a generally educating role, as, for example, in the case of the children's book *Tori no apato* (The apartment of the birds). In a long explanation, the censor discussed his reasons for suppressing the book, a story about a big bird that took possession of the home of some small birds. A story like that might not be noticed in other countries, the censor explained, but it was not in keeping with democratic principles of respect for private property. The effect on present-day Japanese children would be harmful, according to him. His rejection of the book led to a discussion between PPB and the Civil Information and Education Section, which had been asked for a comment. CIE took a practical point of view, saying that it would be a shame to disapprove of the book, because the publisher had already set up plates for it (a prerequisite for being able to submit anything to censorship). The publisher had also used fine-quality paper, which was still in short supply. CIE did not think that the censor's interpretation of the book would be that of children reading it, nor of their parents. In conclusion, CIE did not want to suppress the book. The publishing company had a good record, suppression would mean waste of good paper, a huge financial loss to the company could be avoided, and Japanese readers would not give the same interpretation as the censor anyway. As a gesture of conciliation toward the censor, CIE added that in the future, similar books would not be approved.[41]

As this example shows, censorship led to discussion not only among censors, but also between different departments responsible for different aspects of the Occupation. CIE was responsible for education, so it was perhaps natural that its advice was sought on a question of the impact a certain book would have on children. Material about the atomic bombings of Hiroshima and Nagasaki also required opinions from a number of other agencies, not only in the Occupation Headquarters, but also in the United States.

The censors did not always agree in their judgments. The American journalist William Coughlin described the atmosphere of distrust and disgust that Americans often felt toward the Japanese media: "The Japanese broadcasters continued their outpouring of propaganda, ignoring the Supreme Commander's order. Domei began faking incidents involving American troops and these stories received wide play in the Japanese newspapers."[42] He pointed out that there was a difference between censorship in the beginning and later, due to the fact that at first the censors were army press section personnel, mostly former newspapermen who had been drafted into the war. But after the war ended they were demobilized and returned to the United States, and their place was taken by less experienced personnel, young military men with no newspaper experience. The result was slower work and more confusion. The work was further complicated by imprecise working rules:

> as the examples of the articles which were censored indicate, the censoring officers put the broadest possible interpretation on the press code and went far beyond its original intent. It is apparent that General MacArthur, through his censors, sometimes used his power over the Japanese press for reasons which even the most ardent MacArthur booster would have trouble explaining in terms of Occupation necessity. Sometimes the snipping of the censors' shears appears to have been motivated by political reasons.[43]

An example of censors disagreeing is the case "The Battleship *Yamato*," a poem, written by a former radar officer. The *Yamato*, the largest battleship in the Japanese Navy, was sunk off the coast of Kyushu in 1945. Of the crew of more than three thousand, only a few hundred survived, one of them the author of the poem. The poem dealt with the sinking of the ship and was suppressed on the ground that it was militaristic. But the censor added a footnote to the effect that the poem had first been passed, and that the examiner who passed it was Japanese. "Why?" the American censor asked. He answered: "the Japanese in the examiner must have been inclined to be the most lenient he or she thought the duty of an examiner could allow him or her to be."[44]

Some censors, in fact, protested against the censorship rules. In one case, a small group even sent a formal protest to their superiors, criticizing the key log concerning the new Japanese constitution. The protesters wrote that censorship was suppressing articles that were only of a mildly controversial or a noncontroversial nature. They questioned the legality of the key log itself. According to it, any inference that the constitution had been forced on the Japanese should be suppressed. They were of the opinion that this was against the most basic statements of the goals of the Occupation, the Potsdam Declaration, and the White House Statement on Occupation Policy in Japan, issued on September 6, 1945. It was also contrary to those SCAPINs that decreed an absolute minimum of restrictions on freedom of speech. "SCAP is taking a hypocritical course of action," the protesting censors wrote, and they added that in case the policy of SCAP had changed, a special decree should be issued to let the Japanese know that they were not allowed to discuss their constitution freely.[45]

From the outset, it was clear to the censorship authorities that it would be difficult to set up definite rules for what should and should not be censored. Despite the detailed lists of watchwords sent out by the War Department and others, the agency in charge of the actual censoring—the Civil Censorship Detachment— warned the censors that "censorship is a matter of judgment."[46] CCD did not have "a policy, but many of them, written and unwritten, some of which changed from day to day, and were based upon censorship experience and current developments of the occupation."[47] When a district asked whether very small publications should be censored, it was told a definite, ironclad policy would not be feasible.[48] In some areas the censors might not even be helped by keeping up-to-date with the current interpretation of the rules themselves. This concerned at least information that disturbed public tranquility: "In the last analysis [those] will be subjects that the Supreme Commander does not desire discussed."[49]

This policy was formally in accordance with the commands that gave MacArthur personally, as supreme commander, control over censorship in all respects except its termination.

One example of how interpretation of the rules were changed by SCAP is "criticism of Allied powers." According to the Press Code, the Japanese were not allowed to publish anything that was strongly critical of the Allied powers, including the Soviet Union. When *Hiroshima shimbun* wanted to publish an article in 1946 headlined "An Escape from Vladivostok," therefore, it was refused. The article contained the following sentence: "privation and destitution took a quick toll of our fellow men and by the time of our escape in March the number had decreased to 2,000 men." The censors objected, calling it a violation of paragraph 3 of the Press Code, which prohibited false or destructive criticism of the Allies.[50]

Two years later, the situation both internationally and in Japan was different. The cold war was developing, and the reversal in American Occupation policies meant that leftism was discouraged. There were no further American attempts to protect the Soviet Union from criticism. On the contrary, there was a memorandum to the opposite effect. From September 20, 1948, the phrase "strongly critical of the Allied powers" would not include the Soviet Union. Material that was primarily critical of the Soviet Union would not thereafter be called a flagrant violation (the stiffest rating by the censors).[51]

At different stages there were American suggestions that the basis for censorship should be revised in one direction or the other. In May 1946 the general impression was that the number of censored stories had decreased; no newspapers had been suspended since December the previous year. But a SCAP official informed Coughlin that there were good reasons for maintaining the strict censorship: "While substantial sections of the Japanese press have subscribed to SCAP censorship codes, there are numerous indications that the time has not yet arrived for the relaxation of censorship regulations. Attempts at justification of the Japanese war position continue. The press is now beginning to hint that heavy reparations for Japan are unfair."[52]

Suggestions to terminate censorship were motivated in different ways. For instance, a memorandum from CCD in 1949 suggested that censorship never should have been called censorship at all. Censorship was repulsive to Americans, and "so-called liberty-guardians" had used and misinterpreted it to the detriment of the Occupation. The writer therefore recommended that the Civil Censorship Detachment should be renamed the Communications Surveillance Group.[53] His suggestion, however, was not followed.

At the outset, those who wanted a revision of the Press Code were not successful either.[54] But the thought that precensorship should give way to postcensorship began to take root and was gradually put into effect. One of the motivations brought forward in the early discussions was that with postcensorship, the Japanese themselves would carry the responsibility for conforming to the codes.[55] They could still be checked and punished, but a "responsible" Japanese press would be developed. Also, according to the highest intelligence officer in SCAP, the G-2 chief General Charles Willoughby, the maximum benefits to be derived from close censorship supervision had already been achieved by October 1946. He suggested that SCAP should place full responsibility on the press to, as it were, censor itself. A suitable time to start would be one day before the new Japanese Constitution went into effect. The only reservation he had was that earlier censorship regarding a few sensitive areas, such as public tranquility and criticism against the Occupation and the Allies, ought to remain.[56]

Even with these important qualifications, Willoughby's idea was not accepted at the time. But gradually some changes were made. In the spring of 1946, local broadcast stations had been allowed to transmit sporting events on a postcensorship basis.[57] In the fall, some minor newspapers and news services were transferred to postcensorship because they were not large enough to warrant censorship.[58] The same fall, all precensored newspapers and news agencies were allowed to carry sporting news, advertisements, weather reports, and the like, censored after publication.[59] The bunraku puppet theater and the classical kabuki theater were converted to postcensorship in early summer of 1947.[60]

Several reasons were given for these relaxations. In the case of the puppet theater, it was because this art form had a cultural and historical background, but also because it had "extremely limited audiences."[61] In other cases, such as minor publications, it seems to have been because precensorship had become too cumbersome for the censors.[62]

In the summer of 1947, a comprehensive revision of censorship went into effect. A large number of newspapers and magazines were put on postcensorship.[63] In August, broadcasts were included, although material concerning the Allied powers and the Occupation still had to be submitted for precensorship.[64] During the following month, broadcasts were closely checked and found to have performed satisfactorily. Only two-tenths of 1 percent of the broadcasts were disapproved.[65] Newspapers and magazines were not quite so obedient, however. In October, four months after their change of status, two newspapers and fifteen magazines were reverted to precensorship for "noncompliance." Four newspapers and 511 magazines continued to be censored after publication, however, so most magazines may be said to have followed the rules.[66]

On July 15, 1948, a decision to end precensorship was taken in Washington.[67] It was approved by the president later the same year.[68] There was no announcement, but the editors of all the larger newspapers and news agencies were called to the CCD and told that "they were now believed to completely understand the objectives of the censorship policy." From this time on, they were told that they were to operate it themselves since "General MacArthur now had 'full confidence' in their willingness and ability to do so."[69]

The termination of precensorship did not mean that censorship in general was eased. Japanese publishers worried about what would happen if they broke the rules, now that they had to decide for themselves what was allowed and what was not. *Mainichi* warned its reporters in a confidential memorandum: "Responsibility will be even heavier now that GHQ will not actively enforce censorship prior to publication; it will be more difficult because we will have to keep worrying even after publication."[70]

For the censors themselves, the end of precensorship of mass media did not necessarily mean less work. Instead, PPB expanded its activities in other censorship areas, such as intelligence gathering and analysis. This was done by surveillance of telephone, telegraph, and postal communications of private citizens. That this was no side-business can be understood from the statistics of four million intercepts during one single month. Interest was mostly concentrated on comments regarding violence, strikes, Communist activities, "or any other developments which were of a subversive or possibly subversive nature."[71] The censors were now more concerned about Communists than about militarists. This was yet another sign of the change of emphasis in Occupation policies.

The end to censorship in Japan came on October 31, 1949, via a statement issued by SCAP. Prior to the statement, discussion had arisen concerning whether it was wise to announce the cessation of censorship when it had been forbidden to mention its existence.[72] In the end, the official history of the Occupation explained: "In consonance with the Commander in Chief's general policy of relaxing all forms of restrictive measures vis-à-vis the Japanese people, all categories of Civil Censorship operations were discontinued on October 31, 1949."[73]

But this did not end American influence over Japanese media. Censorship had, after all, not been the only means to influence information. When the war ended and the Occupation started, one of the most important activities of SCAP had been to purge persons regarded as militarists or as tainted by association with militarists. The purge had covered journalists, editors, and media owners, even if it was not until the summer of 1947 that influential wartime publicists were removed from their positions.[74] As in politics and labor organizations, many leftists rose to prominence during the early Occupation. This was true not only among those who had spent the war years in prison, but also among young people, who were inspired by the education in freedom and democracy that they received from the Americans.

In the beginning of the Occupation, leftists were encouraged as a counterweight to the old rightists and militarists, but gradually they came to be seen as a threat. In 1949 and 1950, SCAP instigated the so-called Red Purge. A total of 20,997 alleged Communists and sympathizers lost their jobs, not only in government but also in private industry and the mass media.[75] Despite the dismantling of censorship, neither press nor speech was totally free even during the last part of the Occupation.

As a whole, control through censorship had been accomplished in two phases. Phase one comprised the first months of the Occupation, when the Japanese press made "scurrilous and defamatory attacks" on the Occupation in a "torrent of open slander." The Japanese were brought "to their senses" through punishment.[76] Phase two involved employing censorship as an educational as well as preventive device, according to CCD's own analysis.[77] It was also the period when the difficulties of censorship became clearer. One problem was the sheer cost of paying for the large staff of civilians demanded for the operation. As the rules changed from precensorship to postcensorship, work routines changed from inspection of a large amount of material to spot-checking. This made censorship less all-encompassing, but also less effective. More and more items that earlier would have been suppressed or deleted could be published, even if it was at the risk of unknown punishment for the publisher. The Japanese public also had growing access to material from abroad. Gradually, it became more and more difficult for the Americans to control the image of the world in the minds of the Japanese.

But censorship was not discarded in a mood of hopelessness. Rather, its mission was regarded as accomplished. Japan had been completely demilitarized, and the Japanese government could now take on increased obligations because of the social and political reformation of the country. Extensive surveillance by the Occupation forces was no longer necessary. "The character of the occupation has gradually changed from the stern rigidity of a military occupation to the friendly guidance of a protective force."[78]

Taking into account the ineffectiveness, haphazardness, and adaptability of censorship rules, it hardly seems credible that it was thanks to censorship that Japan developed satisfactorily. Rather, it had made both Japanese mass media and Occupation censors unsure of themselves. To avoid trouble, costs, and possible punishment, Japanese publishers most likely refrained from printing what they thought might be questionable material.

The censorship authorities, on their part, scathingly criticized the four-year censorship operation in the *History of the Civil Censorship Detachment*, pointing out a large number of weaknesses in both planning, organization, and practice. They called the Press Code a catchall to cover and forbid any news items authorities wanted suppressed, for whatever reason. Many provisions gave no guidelines at all as to what specifically was forbidden. The paragraph forbidding anything that might disturb public tranquility was especially criticized: "all news items are designed to prick and disturb 'public tranquility.' Any news item that did not do so would not be read."[79] As a recommendation for future censorship operations, the unnamed author of the official *History* suggests hiring personnel who are not "culls and castoffs," and using satisfactory equipment. Above all, any future Press Code should be concise and explicit, more rigid than elastic, and allow no exceptions. It should not be used as a means of censoring material whose suppression is desired by other military agencies but that is otherwise unobjectionable. Finally, censorship should not be called censorship. Censorship draws criticism. It is never possible to censor everything. Censorship can never control, only spot-check, the author states.[80]

What censorship could do, and did, was to keep certain items out of the public mind and media for a certain time. The reasons for doing so did not necessarily have anything do to with the democratization of Japan.

PUNISHMENT FOR VIOLATIONS

ACCORDING to the Basic Plan for Civil Censorship in Japan, violations of censorship rules could be punished by military tribunal.[1] The Supreme Commander had the responsibility for all phases of censorship operations except their termination.[2]

To bring every violator of censorship rules to court was hardly feasible, and this form of punishment was seldom used. In fact, when censorship activities began it was established that the penalty for violations was suspension.[3] The decision to punish by suspension was taken on the basis of an analysis of the first three days of censorship. The CCD concluded that there were too many violations, and that the leading newspapers and the radio "continued the former propaganda line," linking announcements of Japanese atrocities during the war with outrages by American soldiers in Japan. As a result, they were warned by CCD. Three days later the first suspension went into effect, when *Asahi* was closed down for two days for having stated that the use of the atomic bomb was a war crime, violating international law.[4]

Similar punishment was meted out soon thereafter, when *Tokyo keizai shimbun* was confiscated. Suspension meant a financial loss to the newspaper in that there would be no papers, and thus no income, for as long as the suspension lasted. Confiscation was even more severe, because scarce, valuable paper was wasted.

During the war, under Japanese censorship, allocation of paper

had been an effective way of controlling news. Only media regarded as trustworthy by the Newspapers' and Publishers' Association received paper. In October 1945, SCAP ordered the
Japanese government to eliminate this control over the distribution of paper. But general control over paper allocation was not
eliminated. Instead, the government was instructed to create a
new paper-rationing organization.[5] POLAD, the State Department
representative in Japan, was enthusiastic about paper rationing as
a way of controlling the press. He regarded this as a "most
potent weapon to enforce cooperation by the old established papers." He was of the opinion that in this way not only could the
old established papers be controlled, but new papers would not
be prevented from taking up publishing. He thought that this
method of control was "superior in many ways to censorship."[6]
Japanese saw paper allocation in a somewhat different light, however. In a roundtable discussion report, for example, a Japanese
reporter complained that only papers already established when the
Americans arrived received paper. To his mind, these publishers
had only "repainted their signboards with Democracy," and in
fact were the same ones who earlier had cooperated with the
militarists.[7]

The most lenient way of dealing with censorship violations
was to issue a warning to the publisher. In such a warning the
responsible publisher or editor might be told that the breach was
very serious, and that, if it were repeated, there might be "possible consequences." The publication would subsequently be
closely scrutinized, kept on file, and possibly suspended in the
future.[8] Sometimes the local censorship office offered to explain
the terms of censorship more clearly, in case they were not fully
understood.[9]

The possibility of stricter censorship was used as a threat, both
in the beginning of censorship operations and later, especially
after most media were transferred to postcensorship. At the first
meeting of the Civil Censorship Detachment with publishers in
September 1945, the Japanese were told that, because of their

lack of adherence to SCAP publishing rules, they were to be put on stricter censorship.[10]

When the news outlets in Tokyo, including twelve newspapers and three news agencies, were told in 1948 that they would be transferred to postcensorship, their first question was whether violations meant that they would be returned to stricter censorship. They were told that there was no decision on this matter "since violations were not expected."[11]

That violations did take place, and that they would be punished, became increasingly clear during the following months. One form of punishment was return to precensorship. This could be combined with an order to withdraw all copies already distributed of material that had been deemed objectionable under postcensorship.[12]

From an American point of view, it seems the censorship system worked best during the period when there was both pre- and postcensorship. Then a publication could be put on postcensorship for good behavior (at the same time as the workload of the censors was diminished), but there would always be possibility of returning it to precensorship. "The possibility of being returned to precensorship status was sufficient incentive to keep most postcensored publishers in line with the Press Code."[13]

But this control by uncertainty largely disappeared when almost all media were transferred to postcensorship. The result could be seen immediately. The monthly violation rate in newspapers was five times as great, in books twenty times as great, and in magazines twice as great as before.[14] How to deal with these violations in postcensored material became a problem.

The earlier warnings and the possibility of precensorship still existed,[15] but prosecution in military tribunal now became a subject for discussion within SCAP. According to the initial censorship instructions issued to SCAP, censorship violations could be punished by military court. This had occasionally been done in the early years. One example was two motion picture distributors in Tokyo, who were sentenced to fines and suspended sentences for having illegally exhibited movies in 1946.[16] The same summer, a distributor of kamishibai paper pictures in Osaka was fined and sentenced to prison for having placed a forged censorship stamp on his production.[17] In August, the editor and some employees of China International Press were charged with flagrant violation of censorship. They received sentences consisting of fines and, in the case of one Chinese national the penalty involved deportation to Taiwan.[18]

But censorship trials were by no means common. It was not until a larger number of censorship violations developed in 1948 in connection with less precensorship that the possibility of prosecution was seriously discussed within SCAP. In April 1948, the Civil Information and Education Section suggested to the Intelligence Section G-2 that a publication that had been found to violate censorship regulations on a number of occasions should be arraigned before Provost Court for consideration of whether further publication should be permitted.[19]

G-2 was not enthusiastic, for several reasons. Such trials would mean a step backward in the progress toward a free press, it said. In particular, it worried about the impact such arraignments would have on American correspondents. They were sure to criticize the move, especially if the initiator were the Civil Censorship Detachment.[20]

CCD, for its part, was irritated by articles criticizing the repatriation program of Japanese soldiers from the Soviet Union. It regarded those critical articles as "trial balloons" planted by Moscow propaganda to see "how far they can go in criticism of SCAP under the new system of postcensorship." A prosecution would "effectively demonstrate the teeth of postcensorship," it was believed.[21]

By February 1949 a joint conference was called, with participants from G-2, the Civil Information and Education Section, the Legal Section, and the Civil Censorship Detachment, to discuss the Press Code violations. Many instances of "flagrant" violations were discussed, as well as the fact that "no action has been taken to prosecute offenders.'' Statistics were presented showing that, from June 1 to November 30, 1948, there had been 148 flagrant violations. No less than 47 conferences had been held with publishers to discuss these violations. It was noted that most of the violations had occurred in newspapers of limited circulation, ''often with left-wing or Communist tendencies.'' The joint SCAP conference thought it was possible to discern a pattern in the violations, with ''virulent criticism of the United States and its free enterprise system'' as well as of the Occupation. Individually, the violations were not so serious, but collectively they were. The problem was, how to deal with the situation. Not even suspension was regarded as feasible any more, because it would cause ''adverse publicity in the foreign press.'' Punishment might lead to criticism by foreign correspondents that post-censorship in fact was more severe than precensorship.[22]

As a result, it was recommended that individual units look for violations and take action for prosecution. The Joint Board, consisting of the participants in the conference, should assist.[23]

The Joint Board had been established in January 1949 to consider institution of military court prosecution of flagrant violations.[24] It met altogether five times. The discussions centered around which cases would really stand up to judicial prosecution. On April 1, the board scrutinized different violations. In the opinion of the representative of the Legal Section, the violation most suitable was an item from *Akahata*, the organ of the Japanese Communist Party. The article in question had reported about assemblies in various areas. ''From a legal standpoint'' this item could ''most successfully be prosecuted.'' The condition was that actual rioting would have to have taken place in the course of assemblies. Supposedly *Akahata* could then be accused of having published material that disturbed public tranquility.[25]

At a meeting later the same month, CCD underlined that if any case was taken to court, it must be a clear-cut issue, and public opinion must be strongly behind the case. CCD did not think legal action against leftists would be successful under the present Press

Code. To change the Press Code itself was not feasible, because such an action would draw criticism from civil liberties groups for not relaxing censorship.

Taking such factors into account, it was recommended that of the thirteen cases studied, the one most likely to succeed would be an item from a publication called *Emancipation News*, a Korean News Service outlet. An article headlined "Everlasting Friendship Between the Korean and the Russian People" was regarded as "sufficiently clear-cut" for legal action, being a "clear-cut attack on the U.S. Army." After a short trial, the editor, a Korean named Kim Won Kyun, was, indeed, convicted of having violated the Press Code by attacking the American Occupation Forces, claiming that they "had enforced general elections and massacred opponents." He was sentenced to a stiff five years of hard labor and deportation to his "native" Korea.[26] Another Korean, in a later case, was sentenced to two years in prison.[27]

In a third case a Japanese editor stood accused. The trial became the forum for a discussion on the responsibilities of an editor. Shichiro Morioka of the Associated News Overseas Edition, a news service, defended himself by saying that he had only published news "truthfully and impartially," and that he could not be held responsible for the content of items that were credited to other sources. The accusation concerned material circulated by the Soviet news agency TASS, in which the British were said to have tortured and executed fifteen thousand Malayans, and Japan was said to be a base for invasion of the Far East by Occupation forces. The military court refuted Morioka's argument, saying that an editor was responsible for material appearing in his publication regardless of its source, since he had complete freedom of selection from abundant news sources. Morioka received a sentence of two years' hard labor.[28]

All censorship operations were disbanded October 31, 1949, but two more cases were taken up in court and decided just before the end of censorship. They concerned two leftist publications, which published articles deemed critical of the Occupation. The responsible editors received sentences of two years' imprisonment.[29]

That the Joint Board took up so small a number of cases during its ten months of existence was not due to lack of intention. Rather, the reason was that it was difficult to make a case of what the Occupation authorities felt were violations. ''The Press Code had not been designed to serve as the basis for legal action.'' They did not want to take up any case on which they were not sure of conviction because ''it was the unanimous opinion of the board that the loss of a Press Code prosecution would have had more serious consequences in an Oriental country where the loss of face is all-important than would the failure to take direct action against borderline cases.'' The few but sure convictions were also meant to have ''the effect of keeping other producers in line.''[30]

Whatever the violations, publishers could never be certain whether their items would pass censorship or lead to punishment, possibly even years of hard labor. It is not difficult to imagine that, because of this, Japanese publishers were apt to practice extensive self-censorship. It is also clear that the Occupation authorities relied on their anxiety.

8

CENSORSHIP OF THE ATOMIC BOMB

At 5:29 P.M. on September 14, 1945, the Japanese news agency Domei was prohibited by the Civil Censorship Detachment from sending out any news for twenty-four hours. In a statement to the Japanese press (which relied on Domei for practically all information from Tokyo and abroad) CCD explained that Domei had disseminated news that disturbed public tranquility.[1] On September 18, one of the largest newspapers in the country, *Asahi shimbun*, was suspended for two days for violating the Press Code. SCAP issued the Press Code the same day, in the form of instructions—a SCAPIN—to the Japanese government.[2] This document, along with earlier instructions from SCAP to the Japanese press formulated in a decree of September 10,[3] stressed that no false or destructive criticism of the Allied Powers or the Occupation forces was allowed, and that there was to be no information about troop movements. Public tranquility was not to be disturbed. News had to be true.

What, then, had brought suspension on Domei and *Asahi*? During the Occupation nothing could be printed about the existence of and the reasons for censorship, but an American history of censorship in Japan written for the Civil Censorship Detachment gave the reason as follows: Domei had disseminated a report that included the sentence, "Japan might have won the war but for the atomic bomb, a weapon too terrible to face and one which only barbarians would use."[4] Similarly, *Asahi shimbun* had published an article by Ichiro Hatoyama, a leading politician who later became prime minister. He called the use of the atomic bomb a war crime and a violation of international law: "So long as the United States advocates 'might is right,' it cannot deny that the use of the atomic bomb and the killing of innocent people is a violation of international law and a war crime worse than an attack on a hospital ship or the use of poison gas."[5]

Two days later, on September 17, *Asahi* commented editorially on American reports of Japanese atrocities in the Philippines. It said that if it was true that Japanese outrages cost them the support of the Filipinos, "this point applies also to the Allied forces now in Japan." It also said that the reason the atrocity report was released was to overshadow press reports in Japan of outrages committed by American soldiers there. These two reports plus what was called "propaganda-tinted headlines and slanted foreign news" led to the suspension.[6]

These suspensions were the first instances of U.S. disapproval of Japanese references to the atomic bombings of Hiroshima and Nagasaki. But even before the civilian censorship operations for Japan started functioning, the Occupation authorities made it abundantly clear that material from Hiroshima and Nagasaki was to be strictly controlled. If necessary, reports could be denied even if they were true. The Australian journalist Wilfred Burchett, who wrote for the *London Daily Express*, had firsthand experience with this policy. As the first foreign journalist to reach Hiroshima, arriving before even the first official American delegation, he had traveled alone by overcrowded train from Tokyo. His journey was quite unnerving. Many of the Japanese on the train, in particular demobilized soldiers, seemed hostile toward this unfamiliar Westerner. After a journey of twenty-four hours Burchett arrived on the morning of September 3 in Hiroshima. With the help of a journalist at the local Domei office and, absurdly enough, the local head of the Kempeitai (secret police), he toured the remains of the city and conducted interviews. At one point he actually ran into the first American delegation, which included some journalists. Burchett had no high regard for these colleagues, whom he saw as being totally in the hands of the official information officers. He later accused them of not having had any contact with the local population. The distrust was mutual: they refused to let him fly back to Tokyo with them.

Burchett was able to get his story out quickly nonetheless. The local Domei journalist helped him to send it by Morse code to Tokyo, where it was forwarded to London and published on September 6 as the first foreign eyewitness report from Hiroshima under the headline, ''30th Day in Hiroshima: Those who escaped begin to die, victims of THE ATOMIC PLAGUE 'I Write this as a Warning to the World' DOCTORS FALL AS THEY WORK Poison gas fear: All wear masks.'' Burchett wrote:

> In Hiroshima, 30 days after the first atomic bombing destroyed the city and shook the world, people are still dying, mysteriously and horribly—people who were uninjured in the cataclysm—from an unknown something which I can only describe as the atomic plague. . . . many people had suffered only a slight cut from a falling splinter of brick or steel. They should have recovered quickly. But they did not. They developed an acute sickness. their gums began to bleed and then they vomited blood. And finally they died. All these phenomena, they told me, were due to the radioactivity released by the atomic bomb's explosion of the uranium atom.

Burchett's text was clear. He told about the destruction, the illness, and the hopelessness. When he returned to Tokyo on September 7, he found that he was the center of American official anger. He had to go straight to a press conference called by the deputy head of the Manhattan Project, Brigadier General Thomas Farrell. The main point was to refute Burchett's charges that people in Hiroshima were dying from radiation effects. Farrell explained that the victims Burchett had seen were hurt by the bomb's blast and suffered burns. The Japanese doctors were incompetent to treat them and lacked medicines. When Burchett insisted that fish in the rivers were also still dying, he was told:

"I'm afraid you've fallen victim to Japanese propaganda."[7]

At the time, Burchett did not think of his difficulties with the Hiroshima reporting as anything but ordinary obstruction by officials. In later years he pieced together his whole experience and became convinced that it was part of a pattern that was designed to hide the effects of the atomic bomb. After his visit, Allied journalists were denied permission to visit Hiroshima for some time.[8]

For Japanese journalists, information from the bombed cities and discussions about the effects of the bomb were checked, held, suspended, or deleted for four years. The practices, reasons given, and even decision makers changed. There was never a key log saying that material about Hiroshima and Nagasaki should be deleted from all publications, and news items and books about Hiroshima and Nagasaki did occasionally appear. Because the censorship was not total, it is important to see what aroused the interest of the censors, what action was taken, and why.

A good example is the little book *Masako taorezu* (Masako does not collapse). On March 18, 1947, a member of the American military government team in Nagasaki, Captain Irvin W. Rogers, wrote a letter to the Civil Censorship Detachment in Fukuoka concerning two Japanese books in manuscript form that he had read. On behalf of the team he said that he had found nothing censurable in the manuscripts, that they were worthy of publication and, what's more, that they were true and gripping depictions of a vivid personal experience of the atomic bombing of Nagasaki. One of the manuscripts, *Masako Does Not Collapse*, was written by the fifteen-year-old Masako Ishida. The other was written by her father, Hisashi Ishida, in the form of a story told to his son. On an attached sheet the commanding officer, Lieutenant Colonel Victor E. Delnore, added that the team felt the books were an important depiction of the terrifying experience of living in Nagasaki when the atomic bomb exploded. "They show the reactions of the members of one small family in the holocaust; they show the heartbreak and the pain." For

Delnore the books had an importance beyond Nagasaki: "For us to properly realize the significance of the atomic bomb, to experience vicariously the feelings that so many thousands of Japanese people experienced is desirable in these propitious times."[9]

The district censor in Fukuoka replied formally that it was not the policy of his office to censor books in manuscript form. The publisher should submit two copies of the galley proofs when they were ready. The manuscripts were returned.[10]

Masako Ishida, her father, and Captain Rogers did not give up. Three months later Rogers sent another letter, this time very terse. He was sending two copies of a novel about the experience of a young girl during the atomic bomb explosion in Nagasaki on which he requested the opinion of CCD. The letter was accompanied by signatures of Nagasaki citizens who were in favor of publishing Masako's account.[11] This time the district censor gave a lengthy answer. He explained that he had not taken action earlier because the manuscript "was said to be merely for the personal record of the writers' family." He went on to quote some examples of how the book "very graphically" tells about Masako's experiences of the atomic bombing.

> Flesh raw from burns, bodies like peeled peaches. . . . I was out of my mind. . . . The river was filled with corpses, legs . . . dead bodies of mother and child . . . as if in the Inferno. . . . At last we were defeated in war and I felt mortified. I never could convince myself that it was our sky through which the B-29's carried that devilish atom bomb.

The censor then recommended suppression, "at least for the time being." He referred to the Press Code and the paragraph that mentions public tranquility: "This District believes that the novel *Masako Taorezu* would disturb public tranquility in Japan and that it implies the bombing was a crime against humanity." The book was stirring and it had historical value, he said, but it ought not to be published in Japan until some undefined future, when it would be less apt to "tear open war scars and rekindle animosity."[12]

Another case concerning a book about the atomic bombing of Nagasaki proved to be more complicated, partly because the Occupation authorities tried to make a deal with the publisher: publication would be allowed if an account of Japanese atrocities in the Philippines were included. This time the writer was not a schoolgirl but a well-connected doctor in Nagasaki, Takashi Nagai. Before the war he had specialized in Roentgen research and received so much radiation that he had contracted leukemia. With his two children he survived the atomic bombing of his home city, but he was in a very poor state of health with no hope for recovery. He decided to spend what remained of his life writing about the atomic bombing. He was especially interested in its significance for human morality, a question that was close to him as a Catholic.[13] In 1947 his publisher in Tokyo submitted *The Bells Toll for Nagasaki* to the censors.[14] It was an eyewitness account of the atomic bombing, especially the destruction of the medical university where Nagai was working at the time. As a doctor, Nagai explained "atomic sicknesses." As a Catholic, he tried to find a reason why the largest Christian city in Japan was the victim: "Is there not a profound relationship between the destruction of Nagasaki and the end of the war? Nagasaki, the only holy place in all Japan—was it not chosen as a victim, a pure lamb, to be slaughtered and burned on the altar of sacrifice to expiate the sins committed by humanity in the Second World War?"

This time the censor did not make his decision on his own. He turned instead to a SCAP department that regularly gave advice on matters of special interest to it—the Economic and Scientific Section. Asked for comments on technical accuracy, ESS had no objections regarding the technical information but suggested further checks and asked the Public Health and Welfare Section for its evaluation. Although PHW answered that it had no objections to the publication of information regarding the physical effects of the atomic bomb on humans, ESS suggested that the Civil Information and Education Section might also be asked for a comment. It seems the censor did not follow that advice; instead he made his own recommendation, one that was contrary to those of the two specialist sections. He suggested that the book be suppressed because it would invite resentment against the United States. The censor particularly mentioned that it described at length the scenes of horror, the great death toll, the painful injuries, the death of medical personnel, and the destruction of medical equipment.[15] The matter finally reached all the way up to the assistant chief of staff, General Willoughby, head of G-2, who ordered the book held for six months because it described the horrors and the great death toll and thus was likely to disturb public tranquility and create ill will toward the United States.[16] As the six-month period was ending, one censor started wondering what would happen next. The publisher soon would be able to publish the book without seeking permission; at the most he risked punishment after publication. Should the publisher be advised that he could publish the book? A note scribbled by hand on a slip for internal communication reads: "Recommend no notice to publisher."[17]

Other people also became involved in the case. Mr. Jiro Hayashi of the Ministry of Communications contacted the censors at the Press, Pictorial and Broadcast Division, explaining that he was a friend of the head of a publishing company that wanted to publish the book both in Japanese and in English. Hayashi and the son of the former premier, Yoshida, had made the translation. Dr. Nagai was extremely anxious to see his book in print before he died, and he was now very ill. The censor, however, had his doubts. He scribbled a note under the sentence about Dr. Nagai's illness: "I wish we could check." He recommended that Hayashi be told that the publishing company he referred to was on postcensorship basis and could publish the book if it felt that it conformed to the Press Code. The responsibility would thus rest entirely on the publisher.[18]

Hayashi persisted in his inquiries and returned to PPB in two weeks to ask for permission once again. There were many factors involved, including money. The dying Dr. Nagai had debts to the publisher, who was also a doctor, and wished to pay them with the money from the book. In addition, there was the complicated problem of paper allocation. In the spring the publisher had managed to get an allocation large enough for printing a thousand copies, but this was forfeited because he had not received censorship clearance. If the book was passed, he would start anew to arrange a paper allocation.[19]

The censors were suspicious. The one who had talked to Hayashi wanted to see if the author was "at death's door"; he thought the "whole book deal" was "fishy" and wanted "to get dope on Mr. Nagai." He suggested that someone who was going to Nagasaki should "check up on him." Alternatively, Dr. Nagai could be put on the watch-list, which would mean that any communications, including mail, where his name was mentioned would be specially watched for by the censors. Someone did check on Nagai. A special investigation of the publishing house showed that three of twenty books it had submitted for censorship had contained violations, consisting of "Criticism of SCAP," "Indirect Criticism of the Occupation Forces," and a "Fraternization Comment." The company was classified as center or slightly right of center and recommended for the watch-list.[20]

The matter passed upward again to the Civil Intelligence Section. General Willoughby was informed of where the matter now stood: the Public Health and Welfare and the Economic and Scientific sections still had no objections, but in the Civil Information and Education Section the chief, Lieutenant D. R. Nugent, decided, after reading only a few pages, that The Bells was "certainly inimical to the objectives of the Occupation and not only would possibly disturb public tranquility immediately but would serve as a constant reminder to the Japanese public of what they had suffered at the hands of the Allies prior to the surrender." It should definitely be kept out of print, he recommended. His memorandum referred to paragraph 2 of the Press Code concerning public tranquility. The printing "now or in the future," he stated, could only arouse anti-American feelings "to a dangerous degree."[21]

General Willoughby was of two minds. Of course it was possible to go ahead and suppress the book on the recommendations from the Civil Intelligence Section. On the other hand, was that wise? The atomic bombings of Hiroshima and Nagasaki were facts of history; censorship suppression could never eliminate those facts. Willoughby, head of what he himself had called "the FBI of the Occupation," wondered if it was really advantageous to keep such facts out of print. Would it not be better to let it be printed now *"while we still have the troops and the police power to* counteract it" (emphasized in original). Otherwise it would "surely" be printed when the Americans had left and when the American influence to counteract undesirable reactions would be completely removed.[22]

The Civil Intelligence Section agreed in part with General Willoughby. *The Bells Toll for Nagasaki* was a well-written book and surely would sell well. The cumulative effect was resentment, not so much against the Occupation or Americans as against war in general. The commentator felt that the atomic bombing was described like a catastrophe such as an earthquake or a tidal wave. Besides, it was not possible to prevent publication of the book indefinitely. "We are in a better position now to neutralize an adverse effect, if there is one, than we would be later on," he stated. Intelligence recommended that it not be suppressed.[23]

The recommendation was forwarded to General Willoughby with an added reservation, however, by Colonel Bratton, Willoughby's subordinate. Bratton noted that the book contained information about the composition of the atomic bomb that might be too close to the mark to justify publication. In addition, there were statements about effects on human beings that might be deleterious. Perhaps, Bratton stated, the whole matter should be referred to the Department of the Army in Washington.[24]

At CCD it was eventually decided that there would be no censorship action taken at all, until G-2 or the Department of the Army sent further instructions.[25]

In the meantime, Dr. Nagai was visited by a representative of the district censor. It became clear that he was indeed quite ill. Nagai stated his reason for having written *The Bells Toll for Nagasaki:* Much had been written about the atomic bombing of Hiroshima, and American sympathy had been aroused. He wanted to attract American attention and sympathy to Nagasaki as well, for he felt the bombing of that city was even more significant than Hiroshima. According to the report of the visit, he wanted Nagasaki to get its share of limelight in American eyes.[26]

The matter passed between departments and officers. Colonel Bratton was exchanged for Colonel Tate, having "washed his hands of the matter." The documents are filled with scribbling, including Tate's *"God damn it"* jotted on a slip about the matter.[27] Mr. Hayashi did not let the matter rest. He once again came to the Civil Censorship Detachment, asking if any decision had been made. He added that he understood it might take some time because of the topic.[28]

In March 1948, almost one year after the first submission, General Willoughby demanded action. The publisher was to be offered a deal: he was to be allowed to publish *The Bells* on the condition that he add as an appendix a story called "The Sack of Manila."[29] The publisher was hesitant; he wanted to consult with his editors.[30] After a few days he answered that he did not want to include the Manila story because "the purposes of the two publications are entirely different." The story about Manila disclosed the inhumanity of Japanese militarism and caused the Japanese people, who, he said, had been dragged into war by aggressive militarists, to search their hearts. *The Bells*, on the other hand, saw the dropping of the atomic bomb as divine providence and the beginning of peace for mankind. "With great meekness the author admits the justification for dropping of the atomic bomb," the publisher stated.[31] The Civil Intelligence Section commented that CCD, CIS, and G-2 were in a position to require simultaneous publication, but that this was not recommended.[32]

Willoughby then developed a new line of reasoning, which, unlike regular censors, he wanted explained to the author. The impression of CIE and CIS, who represented average American readers, was that the book could lead people to conclude that the Americans were inhumane in using the atomic bomb. In view of such impressions, the intentions of the writer were immaterial. If one published the description of a certain act, it was also essential to cover the reasons for this act: "we used the bomb to terminate a war *which we did not start*." The bomb, said Willoughby, was used to retaliate against the barbarism of the Japanese war machine. "If and when American military acts were described (as the bombing), then Jap military acts *that were provocation or motive will have to be shown*" (emphasis in original). The "other side of the story," as Willoughby called it, was to be given, or the book would be suppressed in the future as well. In conclusion, the author should be advised that Willoughby's reasoning was "just as good as his own."[33]

When *The Bells of Nagasaki* finally was published in 1949, it did include "The Sack of Manila." It became an instant bestseller. In February, 1949, 30,000 copies had been sold; by July, the total was 110,000.[34]

The detailed cases of Masako and Nagai make it possible to follow the reasoning behind the decisions to suppress material about the atomic bombings, but they are by no means isolated instances. One censor, for example, objected to an exhortation to a child to "study earnestly and become a great scientist, since your parents were made victims of the atomic bomb." He deleted the second part of the sentence, on the grounds that it would cause resentment of the Allied powers.[35]

Discussions about the future of the world after the atomic bomb and material about peace movements also moved the censors to action. Fears of nuclear war were called "incitement to unrest" when they were expressed as follows: "Who can say positively that tens of thousands of atomic bombs will not be used in future wars. . . . In a few years the powerful countries of

Figure 8. **An Example of a Censorship Discussion within SCAP**

~~RESTRICTED~~

IOM

SUBJECT: Censorship of Book on Bombing of Nagasaki   CAW/90(00458)

FROM: Gen Willoughby   TO: Col Dodge)   Date: 10 Jan 48
                            Col Bratton) Action - IN TURN
                            Lt Col Koster - Follow up
                            Exec Officers - Info   2

    1. Your paragraph 5 c: This is, of course, a potent
paragraph and we can always quote CI&E and "hide behind them".
On the other hand, the atomic bombing of Nagasaki is a fact
of history, that no amount of censroship suppression will ever
eliminate. The question in my mind, is whether it is advantageous to keep it out of print now while we still have the
troops and police power to counteract it or let it be printed
after we have left (and it surely will be printed then) with
undesirable reactions (excepted by CI&E) taking place when our
influence has been completely removed.
    2. Comments desired.

1 Incl   s/ Koster
_ n/c _C.A.W._ _ _ _ _ _ _ _ _ _ _ _

CCD File Copy

FROM: Theater Intell   TO: Col Bratton DATE: 12 Jan 48

    1. The book is well-written and will undoubtedly sell   3
well. However, the cumulative effect on one who has read it
all the way through is perhaps more of an abhorrence of war
in general than of resentment against the Occupation or the
Americans. My impression is one of an account of the catas-
trophic manifestations and effects of atomic explosion handled in the same manner as are catastrophes such as earth-
quakes, tidal waves, volcanic eruptions, etc. We can't prevent the book from being published indefinitely and we are
in a better position now to neutralize an adverse effect, if
there is one, than we will be later on.
    2. Recommend we do not suppress it.

1 Incl: n/c _ _ _ _ _ _ _ _ _ _ _ _ _ _ _ _F.B.D._ _ _ _ _ _ _ _ _ _
FROM: Col Bratton   TO: Gen Willoughby   DATE: 13 Jan 48

    1. I am in agreement with par 1, Comment No. 3 above.   4
However, pages 66-73 contain speculation as to the structure
and composition of this bomb which may be too close to the
mark to justify publication at this time. Furthermore, pages
102-160 contain statements as to effects produced upon personnel
which the DA may not desire released.

~~RESTRICTED~~

Source: File 000.73 Censorship News Articles in Japanese Press 1948, SCAP, box
8519.

the world will have manufactured atomic bombs and will possess them. At the same time we must conclude that these countries will use the atomic bombs with one another in the event of another world war. The bombs will be dropped everywhere, causing terrible damage. . . . This would mean the destruction of mankind and the destruction of civilization."[36]

More positive views of the future were also suppressed: "The discovery of the atomic bomb will make the outbreak of war difficult. The international efforts to avoid wars will be accelerated and Japan will possibly become one of the first-class countries without any armies at all."[37] Why this was determined to be incitement to unrest is not readily apparent, unless the thought of Japan having no army was regarded as angering old militarists. The new constitution, created by GHQ, denounced war and in effect denied Japan offensive military forces.

The peace movement, which centered on the anniversary ceremonies in Hiroshima, was followed with interest by the censors. An article in the Tokyo newspaper *Yomiuri* in June 1948 on the necessity of starting a world peace movement in Hiroshima was suppressed.[38] But a few weeks later the news agency Jiji sent out another story about the worldwide peace movement called "No More Hiroshimas." CCD checked with the Civil Information and Education Section, which took exception to publicizing the movement in the Japanese press. It was particularly opposed to the references to repentance for having dropped the atomic bomb. The deputy chief called the peace movement an acute problem for CIE and added that it was causing much trouble. He recommended suppression of the article. G-2 was not quite so categorical, for practical reasons: Jiji had already published the story, although the censors had marked it "Hold," and if action were taken now, perhaps the Japanese sponsors of the peace movement would inform the American sponsors. The result would be bad publicity for SCAP. It would be best to keep the story out of the papers altogether, but because this seemed difficult, G-2 recommended that it be passed.[39]

The question of peace movements continued to disturb CIE. It was worried about possibly objectionable stories that might appear in connection with the anniversary in Hiroshima. The ceremonies themselves were also a worry. There was reason to believe that material had been written that included calls for American atonement for the Hiroshima bombing. But because demonstrations and speeches did not fall under the jurisdiction of censorship CCD did not intend to take any special measures, such as sending a representative to Hiroshima.[40]

When the ceremonies were over, the Analysis and Research Division of the Civil Intelligence Section analyzed the content of articles written during the three-day Peace Festival. It noted that *Yomiuri* had carried an article by the nestor of Japanese nuclear physicists discussing whether atomic power would bring peace or misery to the world. *Asahi* had reviewed the progress of rehabilitation in Hiroshima and Nagasaki. The third major paper, *Mainichi*, had expressed hopes that the Japanese would be "the first and the last people who knew the power of the atomic bomb on the battlefield." In addition, four papers had given brief notice to the festival.[41]

Despite the lack of censorship of the peace movement in Hiroshima in 1948, one could not conclude that such movements were all so unfettered. A year later *Minshu shimbun* (Democratic news) was censored for having criticized the United States when it quoted Professor Joliot Curie, chairman of the French Government Atomic Commission, who spoke at a World Convention for Peace. He accused the United States, in connection with the establishment of NATO, of making war preparations in order to prevent economic panic. He criticized those who subscribed to the idea that the United States could win a war in a moment because it possessed atomic bombs. Instead, Curie said, they should know that such a war would bring bloodshed to all, even to its initiators.[42]

Many items about Hiroshima and Nagasaki were passed, however. It is sometimes difficult to see in what respect the published articles or books were different from those suppressed. Sometimes the material was not censored at all. All censorship stations were not fully operational until 1946. Some postcensored material was only spot-checked.

A survey of books published during the period 1945–49 shows marked differences in publications during different years of the Occupation. In 1945 no book about the atomic bomb was published. A reasonable explanation, apart from possible censorship, is that this was a time of extreme deprivation and chaos. In 1946 the first collection of poetry about the bomb was published. It called for peace and resistance to everything that threatened peace. In 1947 three books were published, although one of them only in a secret edition of 150 copies. In 1948 there was one book about the atomic bomb. In 1949 there were thirteen, among them Nagai's *The Bells of Nagasaki* and Masako Ishida's *Masako Does Not Collapse*. Fourteen books on the subject were published in 1950–51, when censorship had ceased. During the years 1952–55, thirty-three books about the atomic bombings were published, among them the first pictures of the destruction to be shown in Japan since the beginning of the Occupation. These appeared in the weekly magazine *Asahi Graph* on the seventh anniversary of the bombing of Hiroshima. By then the Occupation had already ended.[43]

An analysis of 260 issues of the 41 largest magazines during the first half of 1949 indicates the periodicals were much less likely to contain articles on the atomic bomb. Of 4,193 articles studied, only 5 concerned the bombings of Hiroshima and Nagasaki. Most were about or by Dr. Nagai, who that year had three bestsellers on the subject.[44]

Negative stories on the effects of radioactivity had been suppressed from the beginning, as illustrated by the case of the Australian journalist Burchett. Suppressed, for example, was a story reporting conclusions of the American Atomic Bomb Casualty Commission, which was studying the effects of radiation in Hiroshima. This article reported that descendants of atomic bomb victims might be "physical monstrosities," and that sterility and altered genetic pattern might be effects of radiation. The censors called this report "pure supposition."[45] In contrast, stories containing good news were passed by the censors. A report from Nagasaki in September 1946, saying that the survivors of the atomic bomb in that city appeared to be in good health with no apparent effects on their white corpuscles was passed.[46] One year later, a similar story from Hiroshima, citing a doctor there, was also passed. The doctor said that there was no further fear of atomic diseases, and that the scars of those who had had plastic surgery had all but disappeared.[47]

Some compilations by victims were also allowed. The monthly magazine *Chugoku bunka* published a special atomic bomb issue in 1946, for instance. In 1948 the tourist office in Hiroshima published an English-language introduction to the city, *Living Hiroshima*, which included descriptions of the destruction. Since its theme was positive, it passed the censor's desk. Its first page read: "Hiroshima is alive. It is like any other newly rebuilt city with reconstructed buildings and barrack throw-ups. Without knowing this is *the city*, no one can tell there is special significance attached to all this. Hiroshima's revival has been remarkable."[48]

Reports by Americans constituted a special problem for the censors. A story by a United Press correspondent describing life in Hiroshima in 1947 was passed with no objections by either the Civil Intelligence Section or the Civil Censorship Detachment. There were details of the terrible injuries to people, but also statements to the effect that if the Hiroshima doctors had only known how to treat radiation burns, the loss of life would have been smaller. The reporter claimed that victims had not regarded the bombing as an atrocity until foreign publications containing such suggestions reached Hiroshima more than a year after the event. There was greater interest in Christianity than ever before, and a foreign missionary was quoted as saying that the book *Hiroshima* by the American reporter John Hersey, which had caused so much horror in the United States for its description of Hiroshima, was "perhaps too interesting."[49]

More doubtful to the censors was a column by another American United Press journalist, submitted by *Mainichi*. It suggested that American interests would better be served if the United States rebuilt Hiroshima and Nagasaki instead of spending money on a costly, permanent army of occupation. The Civil Intelligence Section thought that this not only implied criticism of the United States for using the atomic bomb but also might be construed as implying that the Occupation was harsh. Suppression might invite criticism from the American press, however, and therefore CIS recommended that the column be passed.[50]

One of the most complicated cases was Hersey's *Hiroshima*. This consisted of long interviews with six survivors. It had originally been published in the *New Yorker* in August 1946 and had made Americans and people all over the world realize the effects of the atomic bombing, perhaps for the first time. *Hiroshima* became a classic and is still available in many languages. In November 1946 the English-language *Nippon Times* in Tokyo asked the Civil Censorship Detachment for permission to publish the account in Japan. *Nippon Times* was in the process of negotiating an agreement with the *New Yorker*, but before it completed the deal, it wanted to know if it would be allowed to print the work.[51]

CCD was of the opinion that Hersey's reportage contained many passages that might create the impression that the use of the atomic bomb was "unduly cruel." Asked for its opinion, the Civil Information and Education Section answered that it did not approve. *Nippon Times*, it said, could not make any agreement with the *New Yorker* since this would be a violation of the Trading with the Enemy Act. As a result, the request was returned without censorship action. CCD could only censor the Japanese press, and Hersey's account was not the property of the Japanese press.[52]

Nippon Times evidently left the matter at that. But in 1948, the

Authors' League of America was quoted in a news story as still awaiting a decision on five books, among them Hersey's, involved in censorship controversy in Japan. More to the point, the league awaited a reply from General Douglas MacArthur, because in April that year it had received a report that the books had been banned by MacArthur himself. MacArthur responded that reports of the ban were not true, because American literature was not censored. The league then sent a cable to MacArthur, asking if his answer was to be taken as a specific authorization for the books to be published in Japan. The story was picked up by the censor on its way to the Tokyo Associated Press correspondent. He inquired: What were the facts? The controversy about American books concerned not only Hersey but also Edgar Snow, who had become famous with *Red Star over China*, an account of his life with Mao Zedong in the caves of Yan'an.[53]

In a telegram to Oscar Hammerstein II, president of the Authors' League of America, MacArthur denied that Hersey's and Snow's books had been banned. He called it ''a maliciously false propaganda campaign aimed at producing the completely fallacious impression that an arbitrary and vicious form of censorship'' existed in Japan.[54] It was not until 1949, however, that the Japanese finally were allowed to read Hersey's *Hiroshima*.[55]

Scientific Atomic Bomb Material in the United States

''Facts about nuclear explosions are born secret,'' wrote Edward Teller.[56] He knew, because he was involved in the atomic bomb program from its beginning. And from the beginning secrecy was a dominant feature of the program. This secrecy was imposed not only on everyone involved in making the bombs, but also on the American press. As early as April 1940 a suggestion was brought up in the National Research Council for a censorship committee to control publication of scientific papers on nuclear fission. Sometime later, when a Reference Committee was set up within the council, the publication policy became much broader and aimed at controlling publication of nuclear material in all fields of possible military interest. Editors were contacted and asked to send in manuscripts that possibly touched on these areas for review by a subcommittee, which would decide whether they should be published or not. This procedure was quite successful, especially since most of the scientists in the United States who worked in the field of nuclear physics were engaged in the atomic bomb program. They were sworn to secrecy and thus unable to submit any papers to scientific journals.[57]

Stricter rules for what was regarded as military information were inaugurated in September 1943 within the Manhattan Engineering District (MED) which developed the atomic bomb. This included classification of material into top secret, secret, and so forth. A censorship review program of newspapers and periodicals was also started. At first, this covered only the leading newspapers and a few magazines, but by spring 1944, 370 newspapers and 70 magazines were being reviewed. This was said to be complete coverage. On December 1, 1943, the Office of Censorship had sent out a censorship code to publishers. They were now checked by MED as to whether they violated the provisions regarding its activities. If violations were detected, they were reported to the Office of Censorship.[58]

As the actual testing and use of the atomic bomb approached, the question of controlling information about it became more acute, as well as more complicated. Secretary of State James Byrnes states in his memoirs that news releases covering every foreseeable contingency were prepared, to be issued only if necessary.[59] These news releases, including the ones that were to be released after the actual atomic bombings, were written by the science editor of the *New York Times*, William L. Laurence. Laurence became a key person for the highly selective information activities of MED. He does not seem to have found his dual role as propaganda officer and journalist bothersome. In the spring of 1945, Laurence had been contracted by the head of the Manhattan Project, Brigadier General Leslie Groves. He drafted several statements to be used after the first test of the atomic bomb, as well as the statement President Truman was to make. His drafts were discussed in the Interim Committee, the specialist committee appointed to advise the president on atomic bomb questions. The committee thought Laurence's statement for the president was too detailed, even phony. It preferred that the president make only a short statement, and the drafting was turned over to another person.[60] But Laurence continued his work as introducer of official facts about the atomic bomb. He was the only journalist who was present when the first atomic bomb was tested at Los Alamos. He was also the only journalist to see any of the atomic bombings, when he was allowed on one of the planes to Nagasaki. His reports became the basis for those of other journalists, for he was the only one with access to the facts.

The Australian Wilfred Burchett felt that Laurence's dual position made both him and his information suspect. Burchett, it will be recalled, had reported on the effects of radiation in Hiroshima when he managed to go there alone as the first foreign journalist. His reports were intensely disputed by the deputy head of the Manhattan Project, General T. F. Farrell, at a press conference in Tokyo on Burchett's return. Farrell had also been to Hiroshima, together with a group of selected journalists. In Burchett's view, this was "undoubtedly intended as a culminating coup in the official management of what had been described as 'the biggest news story in the history of the world.' " Farrell's explanations were published in the *New York Times*, on September 12, under the headline, "No Radioactivity in Hiroshima Ruin." The article read in part: "Brig. Gen. T. F. Farrell, chief of the War Department's atomic bomb mission, reported tonight after a survey of blasted Hiroshima that the explosive power of the secret weapon was greater even than its inventors envisaged, but he denied categorically that it produced a dangerous, lingering radioactivity in the ruins of the town, or caused a form of poison gas at the moment of explosion." The Farrell report corroborated an article by Laurence, which had been published September 9 and was datelined Atom Bomb Range, New Mexico. The purpose was to disprove Japanese accounts of new deaths weeks after the bombings. "To give the lie to these claims," a group of journalists had been allowed into the testing area at Los Alamos. Laurence quoted General Groves as saying: "The Japanese claim . . . that people died from radiation. If this is true, the number was very small. . . . The Japanese are still continuing their propaganda aimed at creating the impression the we won the war unfairly and thus attempting to create sympathy for themselves and [obtain] milder terms, an examination of their present statements reveal."[61] Laurence continued to cover the development of nuclear weapons and was later present at tests at Bikini.[62] He was awarded the Pulitzer Prize and a War Department commendation.

The American press, with some prodding from the Office of Censorship, limited itself to publishing the official story. At the explosion of the first atomic bomb in New Mexico, they thus wrote of "a harmless accident." The local newspapers carried some eyewitness reports, among them of a blind girl who saw light, but they were not pursued further.[63] The journalists who were accompanying President Truman to Potsdam on board the *Augusta* were briefed by the president himself. He made them promise not to divulge the secret. "Here was the greatest news story since the invention of gun powder. And what could we do with it? Nothing. Just sit and wait. . . . The secret was so big and terrifying that we would not discuss it with each other. I locked my notebook on the first atomic bomb briefing in a safe," wrote one of the reporters, Merriman Smith.[64]

When the atomic bombing of Hiroshima took place on August 6, 1945, the press had to make do with prepared statements. In President Truman's announcement of the bombing, he said that normally the American government and its scientists would make "everything about the work with atomic energy" public. But as it was, they would first examine methods to protect the world from the danger of sudden destruction and not divulge processes of production or all military applications.[65] Meanwhile, on the Pacific island of Tinian, about one hundred American journalists waited for the return of the *Enola Gay* and other planes that had participated in the attack on Hiroshima. They were requested to send their stories via Washington for clearance, and they also had inadequate technical facilities to transmit their material. At the suggestion of Farrell, who was responsible for the atomic bomb project on Tinian at that stage, as of the following day, news stories could be cleared on the spot and did not have to be sent via Washington.[66]

The decision to keep secret as much material about atomic power as possible was not made without discussion. From scientists to politicians, opinions varied widely. The most usual arguments were that it would be impossible to maintain secrecy after the war, and that scientific freedom was a democratic right. One example of this view is a memorandum to the secretary of war from Vannevar Bush, head of the Office of Scientific Research and Development, and James Conant, president of Harvard University and chairman of the National Defense Research Council. They called it foolhardy to try to maintain the security of the United States by preserving the secrecy of the atomic bomb. Complete secrecy would not be possible, because many already knew about it and refrained from publishing only because of wartime voluntary censorship. An attempt at secrecy not only would fail, but would make the Soviet Union proceed in secrecy with research. On the other hand, if the world were accurately informed about atomic bombs, in each country "public opinion would have true information about the status of the armament situation. Under these conditions there is reason to hope that the weapon would never be employed and indeed that the existence of these weapons might decrease the chance of another major war."[67]

The pros and cons of releasing information were weighed in connection with the so-called Smyth Report. This was an extensive report of the scientific work of the Manhattan Project, but it did not include anything connected with the actual construction of the bomb. Completed before the bomb was tested, it seems to have been written as a proof that all the money that MED had received during the war (without congressional control) had been spent properly. Such proof might be needed if Congress should inquire after the war, and perhaps also in case the whole atomic bomb project failed.[68]

Immediately after the bombing of Hiroshima a discussion ensued between the president and science members of his Interim Committee dealing with problems of the atomic bomb. These individuals, along with Leslie Groves, chief of MED, were of the opinion that the Smyth Report should be released. It was clear that something had to be reported, and Groves thought the easiest means would be the Smyth Report, which also had been cleared by Great Britain, cooperator in the construction of the atomic bomb. A quick release would be essential in the effort to retain maximum secrecy about the atomic bomb, Groves thought. Secretary of War Stimson did not want to "give away any secret which would really help a rival." The scientists, on their part, thought that publication of this controlled study would prevent the harm that might result from reckless and excited versions, which they were sure would circulate if there was too much secrecy. This argument convinced the president, and the Smyth Report was released by the War Department a week after the bombing of Nagasaki.[69] It was prefaced, however, with the statement, "The best interests of the United State require the utmost cooperation by all concerned in keeping secret now and for all time in the future all scientific and technical information."[70]

On September 14, 1945, the War Department sent out a confidential note to editors in which the president of the United States asked American editors and broadcasters, as well as the American public, to protect the secret of the atomic bomb in the national interest. This, it was explained, was not to impose censorship. Information should be withheld until the editors had counseled with the War Department on subjects such as the scientific process and techniques employed when the atomic bomb was used, uranium, production of bombs, and information about atomic bomb plants.[71] The next day Truman directed the secretaries of State, War, and Navy, the Joint Chiefs of Staff, and the Director of the Office of Scientific Research and Development to take any steps needed to prevent release of information on a wide range of subjects concerning the atomic bomb, unless the president had given specific approval.[72] Two weeks later this was modified. Mention that a certain individual or organization had something to do with the atomic bomb project was now allowed. One could also write about the general nature of the project itself. But any information that could be of value to any foreign government, and which that government could not easily obtain without espionage, was prohibited from being released.[73]

While accepting the regulations, the press discussed the question of secrecy. The day after the Hiroshima bombing, the *Chicago Tribune* had written: "The secret belongs to all the American people. It must be guarded and withheld jealously until they have the proof that those who obviously will want to share it cannot use it to the detriment of this nation." This argument, supported by others, developed into the theory that only an American monopoly on the secret of nuclear arms could protect the world. But in the *Herald Tribune* Walter Lippman wrote: "The object of our policy cannot be to keep the secret. Our object must be to prevent the secret use of the knowledge as a military surprise. To those who contend that we should guard this secret, we must, I believe, reply that on the contrary, the safest course is to guard against its being a secret anymore."[74]

In October the president asked the Joint Chiefs of Staff what they thought about the matter. That was the start of a week-long intense debate between the Joint Chiefs. One of the main questions was whether the Soviet Union should be singled out as a country to which no information about the atomic bomb should be given. After much discussion it was decided not to single out the Soviet Union in the final recommendations. Instead, more positive aspects, such as international control of atomic weapons, would be emphasized. In the final memorandum for the president, the Joint Chiefs stated that free information about the atomic bomb would accelerate the arms race, make the United States vulnerable to atomic bomb attacks, hinder international control of atomic power, and be a sign of weakness.[75]

The policy of publication was made into law with the Atomic Energy Act of 1946. Under "Control of Information," the Atomic Energy Commission was given the power to formulate and control the policy for dissemination of restricted data "in such a manner as to assure the common defense and security." "Restricted data" was defined as "all data concerning the manufacture or utilization of atomic weapons, the production of fissionable material in the production of power." Exceptions were data that the commission had determined could be published "without adversely affecting common defense and security."[76]

Edward Teller's statement remained appropriate: facts about nuclear explosions were born secret. Everything that was not expressly released by the AEC was, a priori, prohibited for publication.

For some time, the all-powerful leader of the Manhattan Project, Leslie Groves, continued to wield power. When Bernard Baruch, the U.S. representative to the United Nations Commission on Atomic Energy, needed some material for discussions on possible international control of atomic power through the United Nations, he was told by President Truman to check with Groves. Baruch was allowed to make only such disclosures as had the prior approval of Groves. Groves's clearance was the same as that of the Atomic Energy Commission, and he received authority to continue as before in relation to declassification.[77]

It was Groves, who, earlier that same year, had brought about a stricter policy within the administration in regard to atomic bomb material. He thought that the Senate hearings and forthcoming navy tests made it increasingly difficult to safeguard classified information on the atomic bomb. Military and naval personnel "of all ranks" were engaged in speculation, and there was risk of a "serious loss of security." This led President Truman to order all departments and agencies of the federal government to stop "uncontrolled discussion." The War Department in its orders to commanders added that public discussion should be limited to information that had been officially released.[78]

But something obviously had to be said about the effects of the atomic bombings of Hiroshima and Nagasaki. When the Japanese news agency Domei in late August sent out reports about conditions in the two cities, they were picked up by Associated Press and United Press. According to these reports 360,000 people had been killed or wounded in Hiroshima, and 120,000 in Nagasaki. The stories told in detail about the destruction of the cities, about the injuries, and about persons who had looked well but now were suddenly dying. The War Department declined to comment.[79]

It was not until February 1946 that the Joint Chiefs of Staff considered the question of what specifically should be released about Hiroshima and Nagasaki. The discussions were caused by a British government question on when and how the United States planned to release the reports of the investigations made in Hiroshima and Nagasaki. The Joint Chiefs now thought it desirable that some information about the effects of the bombings be released. The information should be as factual but and as complete as the security restrictions allowed. Such authentic publicity, it was felt, would help the Japanese understand the relationship between atomic and conventional weapons. It would also emphasize the importance of creating effective controls for atomic weapons. The Joint Chiefs proposed that the release of the American report should be synchronized with that of the British. But four months later they had changed their minds. Excusing themselves in a memorandum to the British Chiefs of Staff, they admitted to not being able to agree among themselves on the matter: "As will be understood by the British Chiefs of Staff, release of information on atomic bombs has become of primary political concern in the United States and hence is not under the sole cognizance of the United States Chiefs of Staff.'' A short time later the Joint Chiefs listed information that they regarded as desirable to withhold. Direct reference to the height of the bomb burst, the effects of gamma ray radiation on the human body, information that indicated effective protection against radiation, as well as direct reference to any information that might make it possible to compute the diameter of the ball of fire of the bomb should not be released. Suggestions for deletions in the British reports followed. The British Chiefs of Staff accepted all of them.[80]

Starting in the spring of 1946, Groves and the Atomic Energy Commission finally started a regular program of declassification of atomic bomb material. Declassification guides were developed, as well as a system for review.[81] But it was not until the end of January 1947 that the first 270 atomic energy papers were declassified. ''These papers constitute the first sizable release of atomic energy information which has been made since the early days of the war when a top-secret classification was slapped on everything having to do with nuclear physics,'' the Department of Commerce announced. Most of the papers dealt with technical questions of a very high scientific level.[82]

The responsibility for release of information rested with the AEC, but only concerning scientific and technical aspects. Material regarding military participation in projects could be released only with approval of the secretary of defense. In this way information about atomic bombings and atomic bomb tests had to be cleared jointly in Washington by the AEC through its Military Liaison Committee and by the Department of Defense.[83]

Japanese Scientific Material

When censorship guidelines mention atomic bombs, atomic energy, and atomic research, they usually attach scientific meaning to it. This is the case with the ''Subject Matter Guide for United States Civil Censorship Operations in All Occupied Areas.''

Atomic energy is simply one of many subjects about which information should be gathered.[84]

At the time of the construction of the atomic bomb testing ground at the Eniwetok atoll in the Pacific, specific key logs were issued for Japan. The first of these, from December 6, 1947, states that there may be no reference to nor comment on the construction or operation of the testing grounds. Everything that was not an official release was to be deleted or suppressed.[85] Three weeks later this was modified. News articles with comments or references made by American or Japanese scientists might be published, subject to several restrictions: They must be general and not contain anything that threatened the security of the United States, including bomb performances, critical mass, details of manufacture, results of bombings, and official reports of scientific interest. They must not contain controversial predictions as to the long-range effect of atomic bombs. The reason given was that, because of the limited number of available facts, one could not make conclusive predictions, and such predictions that were made might "unnecessarily alarm the public."[86]

The key log was accompanied by a note to the censors that material that might come under the key log should be checked with the Economic and Scientific Section under SCAP in every instance prior to action.[87] ESS had a Special Projects Unit (SPU) under the leadership of Dr. Harry C. Kelly that kept surveillance over all sensitive Japanese research that might relate in any way to atomic research. It kept custody of and controlled all radioactive ores, products, and materials in Japan, and it made recommendations to SCAP concerning policies and changes of policies regarding atomic research.[88] SPU thus also had responsibility for deciding whether material concerning the atomic bomb contained information that should be suppressed for scientific reasons, or, as the key log stated, because it threatened the security of the United States.

The matter was not simple. Material might be acceptable for release from some points of view, but not from others. Concern-

Figure 9. **Classification of a Japanese Report on the Atomic Bombings of Hiro-shima and Nagasaki**

TOP SECRET

HEADQUARTERS
U.S. STRATEGIC BOMBING SURVEY
(PACIFIC)
APO 234
C/O POSTMASTER, SAN FRANCISCO

#121
SPU

10 November 1945

INTELLIGENCE MEMORANDUM

TO   : All Divisions

SUBJECT : Japanese Survey of Atomic Bombing of
                  Hiroshima and Nagasaki.

1. This report on the atomic bombing of Hiroshima and
Nagasaki has been prepared at the request of G-2, U. S. Strategic
Bombing Survey, by the Japanese Scientist, Dr. Yoshio NISHINA.

2. Dr. NISHINA leads the "RIKKEN GROUP" of scientists who
have been attempting to develop atomic power. He and his assistants visited both cities shortly following the bombings.

3. Further inquiry may be directed to Dr. NISHINA through
G-2, U.S. Strategic Bombing Survey.

RICHARD KEEVE,
Comdr, USNR,
Chief, G-2,
USSBS.

1 Incl:

TOP SECRET

Source: SCAP, box 8536.

ing the atomic bomb, SPU did not always want to take responsibility. A book might be cleared for publication in the United States, for example, but then be submitted for censorship in Japan and SPU consulted. In a typical case Dr. Kelly would answer that as long as the book was cleared in the United States it could, from his point of view, also be published in Japan. This was the case with the so-called Smyth Report, the summary of the development of the atomic bomb and nuclear physics discussed earlier in this chapter.[89]

Then again, there might be hesitation. In 1948 the Japanese magazine *Choryu* wanted to publish a nonclassified report by the Atomic Energy Commission to the United Nations Security Council in 1946. SPU refused to make a recommendation as to whether it could be published in Japan. Instead G-2, the intelligence chief, would have to give clearance for publication of material that concerned nuclear fission and related topics. Dr. Kelly said that he would not care to make any other recommendation than that material formerly checked with his unit should be forwarded to G-2 for decision. The problem was not solved until G-2 radioed the Department of the Army for advice. He was told that the report had already been released for general publication by the Department of State. Consequently, there was no objection to its being published in Japan.[90]

It is clear there was uncertainty about who was responsible for what. In the last instance, the Supreme Commander of the Allied Forces, General MacArthur, could decide what could and could not be published in Japan. But what should be done with material that might be classified in the United States? Was that also secret in Japan? Who decided about such matters? The Economic and Scientific Section asked these questions specifically of G-2. Did ESS or its Special Projects Unit have the authority to classify, declassify, or change classifications of reports made by Japanese scientists who had researched the results of the atomic bombings of Hiroshima and Nagasaki? G-2 answered, somewhat cryptically, that according to the Basic Intelligence Directive, all information regarding nuclear physics should have a classification no lower than secret, and that the authority to classify was vested in the head of ESS.[91]

This was a short answer to a complicated question that engaged many departments, including CCD, ESS, G-2, SCAP, the Joint Chiefs of Staff, and the Atomic Energy Commission. Most particularly, the question centered on how to handle reports by Japanese scientists and doctors on the results of the atomic bombings.

Many of the doctors themselves were survivors of Hiroshima or Nagasaki; they had collected their material in the ruins during the first weeks and months after the bombings. The material was often unique, since American survey teams did not do any serious research there until later. The Japanese had been there and worked, observed, and collected research material from the very day of the atomic bombing. Their research results were crucial to the knowledge of the atomic bomb's effects on the environment and on human beings. No other such material existed. The reports were written from practically all angles—from burn wounds to sperm and white blood cell counts to late effects of radiation sickness. Research teams of scientists from all fields had hurried to Hiroshima and Nagasaki to record and analyze the effects both on human beings and on the environment. Many of the researchers were well known in their specialties abroad, and many had been educated in the United States before the war.[92] The Japanese scientists were eager to publish their papers and to discuss their findings with colleagues from a scientific point of view. Perhaps most eager to present their observations were the medical doctors. They were battling every day to cure the illnesses caused by the atomic bomb, illnesses and injuries they had never seen before and which they were at a loss how to treat. Only by exchanging information with colleagues could they hope to be able to help their mysteriously dying patients.

One doctor eager to publish was Takashi Nagai, the prominent x-ray scientist and author of *The Bells of Nagasaki*, discussed earlier. Nagai had been on duty at Nagasaki University Hospital when the atomic bomb exploded over the city. Although wounded, he organized his students and hospital staff to help survivors. It was only after some days that he returned to what had been his home. Nagai was aware that he did not have long to live. On the plot where his former home had stood, he settled down in a small hut, not much larger than a sleeping mattress. He named it Nyokodo, "Love-Your-Neighbor-as-Yourself-House." It still exists as a small museum to the memory of Nagai. He was cared for by his children and admirers, who saw him as a missionary for world peace. He became something of a Christian mystic, believing that there was a higher meaning and value in the suffering of the atomic bomb victims. He saw them as sacrifices, necessary to atone for the sins of the war. But the bells, heard across the atomic wasteland, also carried a message of hope and resurrection, according to Nagai. His writings became famous throughout Japan, and the emperor paid him a personal visit. His funeral in 1951 was a notable event in Nagasaki.[93]

As a doctor, Nagai was deeply concerned about the impotence of his hospital staff after the bombing.

> For the first time in history the atom had exploded over the heads of human beings. Whatever symptoms might appear, the fact was that the patients we were now treating had diseases that were completely new in the annals of medical history. To ignore these patients would not only be an act of cruelty toward individual persons, it would be an unforgivable crime against science, a neglect of precious research material for the future. We ourselves were already experiencing in our bodies the first stirrings of atomic sickness. If we continued our rounds without adequate rest, our symptoms would get worse—and we would die. Or even if we didn't die, we would certainly fall seriously ill.
>
> And yet my academic conscience gave strength to my body. "Examine the patients!" it said. "Observe them carefully! Grasp the evidence! Discover the very best method of treatment!"
>
> Such was the constant inspiration I received from my conscience. We had no machines for making experiments, no instruments to make tests. We had no paper and we had even lost our

pencils. We had only some scalpels and pincettes, some needles and a reserve of disinfectants and bandages which we divided out in bags as medical kits. But we had our heads, our eyes, and our hands. With these we would surely achieve something.[94]

A young American navy doctor, Lieutenant Richard B. Berlin, who arrived in Nagasaki in early September 1945, saw the Japanese doctors working in tattered clothes. They were "pitifully ignorant of recent developments in science." They received little or no assistance from the government in Tokyo. The manufacture of medical supplies had ceased because of damage in the air raids.[95] One year later, in August 1946, the American journalist Mark Gayn visited Hiroshima. He was told by a doctor at the Red Cross hospital that people still came in, complaining of a strange fatigue: "Who can tell what it is? . . . Perhaps imagination. Perhaps lack of food. Possibly the result of atomic radiation. We know so little."[96]

All reports in Japanese medical journals were heavily censored. Although they did not have a wide readership, they were scrutinized for criticism of SCAP (twenty instances of thirty-eight), wartime nationalist propaganda (eight), references to censorship (five), and discussion of the effects of the atomic bombs (two). Obituaries were undesirable, even mentions of SCAP officials made out of gratitude. Discussion of mixed-blood children was deleted as "indirect criticism of the occupation."[97]

In spite of censorship, some reports of the atomic bombings did appear in medical journals. Most were published in 1947, when a total of forty-five articles appeared. When censorship ended in 1949, three more articles had been published. The first article, however, was published in October 1945. The author, Masao Tsuzuki of Tokyo Imperial University, became the main liaison between Japanese and American researchers regarding the atomic bomb effects. One part of the article that cited American reports claiming that Hiroshima would be unlivable for seventy-five years was passed by the censors. But another part, speculating that the bombs had contained poisonous gas, was deleted. The censor referred to "disturbance of public tranquility."[98]

In 1948 Toshiko Kobayashi, assistant chief of the Hiroshima workers' section of the Ministry of Labor's Women and Minors Bureau, made a survey of female atomic bomb victims. The findings were shocking, but the report was written in careful, indirect language. SCAP prohibited its publication.[99] The fields of censorship of medical and scientific material seemed to be as wide as in any other area, but there was confusion about what the limits were.

One of the first directives that SCAP issued in Japan prohibited all Japanese research in areas that had to do with nuclear physics.[100] Japanese scientists who were thought to have engaged in such research were taken into custody and the laboratories put under American guard.[101] The scientists were released and could enter the laboratories again in February 1946, but all research activities that involved atomic energy were still prohibited. Lists were established of all scientists and students who had been connected with such research. No publicity regarding these policies and actions was allowed.[102]

In August the United States took up the question of Japanese research with the other Allies in the Far Eastern Commission, asking for a review of the policy that Japanese were not allowed to do atomic energy research. The request was not sufficiently detailed, however, and the policy was not clarified until December. While the United States suggested that atomic energy research of a military nature should be prohibited for Japanese but that other research should be allowed, the other Allies, with the exception of the Indian representative, did not want to change policy. The result was that the Japanese would not "at present" be allowed to do research in any aspect of atomic energy.[103]

Although the United States accepted the decision, it worried about possible criticism resulting from the exclusion of Japanese from a certain field of research, which could be seen as a limit on scientific freedom. The United States had already been subject to such criticism in the fall of 1945 when Occupation officials were looking for proof that the Japanese had tried to develop an atomic bomb of their own. In November, without any warning, Occupation troops destroyed five cyclotrons for research in nuclear physics. The result was heavy criticism from all over the world. On the other hand, the Allies had made a joint decision regarding atomic research in defeated Germany, which had not brought any criticism at all.[104]

It was not until May 1949 that Japanese scientists finally were allowed to take up atomic energy research. Even then, they were excluded from anything that might be directed toward "developments in the field of warlike activities." If in doubt, they should acquire special approval from SCAP.[105] The change of policy was followed by invitations to Japanese scientists to study in the United States and other countries. For the United States, resumed Japanese research meant access to Japan's laboratories in any crisis that might occur because of the intensified cold war.

Curiously enough, the manuscripts of Japanese scientists and doctors describing the effects of the atomic bombings of Hiroshima and Nagasaki were not considered to be connected with atomic energy research.

The first surveys of atomic bomb damage were organized by the Japanese Army on August 6. A survey team from the naval base at Kure, close to Hiroshima, arrived in the city shortly after the bomb was dropped. The first surveys tried to determine the nature of and damages caused by the bomb. The military teams were followed by teams from most national universities. Japanese newspapers reported on the results of the surveys in articles that were subsequently transmitted throughout the world. For instance, *Asahi* wrote on August 29 that "medical science is shaken by the horror of the atomic bomb," detailing how radiation "pierced the flesh" and adding that no treatment or rescue existed. Similar information, transmitted by Domei radio to the American zone, was published in American newspapers. Reports stated that thirty thousand people had died two weeks after the bombing of Hiroshima, and that those still alive were "living ghosts," sure to die from radiation.[106]

The Japanese research teams were organized by the National Research Council of Japan into a Special Committee for the Investigation of the Effects of the Atomic Bomb. This committee had several sections, the largest being the medical one with 150 investigators and 1,000 assistants from almost all large medical schools and hospitals in Japan.

On August 10, Leslie Groves, the head of the Manhattan Project, had named the American delegation that would go to Hiroshima and Nagasaki to survey the results of the bombings. The leaders were T. F. Farrell and J. B. Newman. Medical and structural damage were to be studied, and the group was to verify that there would be no danger from radiation to advancing Allied troops. The question of radiation was particularly sensitive: while the Japanese were claiming its existence, the Americans were denying that their new weapon had such a terrifying, uncontrollable, lingering effect. When Farrell arrived in Yokohama on August 30, he started to organize his teams and their work. On September 3 the Japanese presented their first report on atomic bomb damage to the Americans. It was then decided to combine the Japanese and American surveys. The Japanese clearly had gathered much useful material. On September 6, MacArthur ordered the Japanese government to arrange the delegation's trip to Hiroshima by airplane and to cooperate with Farrell. He also ordered twelve tons of Red Cross relief supplies to be sent to the survivors.[107]

The Japanese committee worked with the Americans from September 1945, submitting its reports to them. The reports, which numbered about eighty at the end of 1946, included such diverse subjects as, lists of where survivors had been found in the days immediately following the bombings, the course of atomic bomb sickness, possible genetic effects, and suggestions for treatment and protection in the light of experience.[108] The Japanese scientists were not always willing to hand over their reports, but they had no choice.[109] They did not always inform the Occupation authorities of research under way.[110] Although there was no prohibition on publication of research results of projects that had been cleared, all papers concerning the effects of the bombings ought to receive prior clearance before publication according to SCAP. In addition, the scientists' "desire for self-censorship was encouraged."[111]

The Japanese scientists were concerned about what was being done with their reports, which often were compiled with great difficulty. Their anxiety was voiced by Dr. Masao Tsuzuki, the secretary of the medical atomic bomb committee of the National Research Council, who was the first guide of American investigators in Hiroshima. In June 1946, he asked permission to publish the reports in Japanese scientific journals. In instructions from the Joint Chiefs of Staff, SCAP was told that he must decide whether the manuscripts might jeopardize the security of the United States, prejudice its relations with a foreign country, or derogate from its advantages in the field of scientific research and development. If the answer was yes, the decision on publication could only be taken by the Joint Chiefs.[112]

Many American individuals and agencies favored letting the Japanese publish their manuscripts, for different reasons. In the fall of 1945, for instance, the president of the National Academy of Sciences, Dr. Frank Jewett, asked the Manhattan Engineering District for a definite policy on the matter. He was concerned that withholding of information would retard medical research on the effect of atomic bombs. He asked General Groves to make available to all concerned all medical and biological material of the Manhattan District and to allow publication of this material.[113] In late 1946, an American commission, traveling to Japan to do follow-up studies on atomic bomb casualties, also recommended that Japanese scientists be allowed to publish their reports. If they were not encouraged to continue their research, the argument went, the result might be a loss of essential material on the casualties of the bomb. There was much information in Japan "for the taking," but it was not possible to get "thorough Japanese cooperation unless we give them an outlet for their work." For instance, the Japanese had protocols of autopsies made of the victims of the atomic bombings, even from the very first period after the bombings. The Japanese doctors should be given credit for cooperation in publications.[114] This cooperation ought to be extended into long-term follow-up studies. Relationships should be established with Japanese medical faculties and universities, and the Japanese scientists should be directed and stimulated to continue their studies.[115]

The chairman of the Army Medical Research and Development Board wrote to Groves that it was only through the stimulus of publication that one could hope to encourage the Japanese to maintain their interest in continuing studies of radiation, especially since it would hardly be possible to bring over American personnel to Japan to do such studies. The United States was thus dependent on the Japanese for long-term studies of those who had experienced atomic bombings. Groves agreed fully, but only as long as the theater commander (SCAP) approved, as long as nothing classified "Restricted" or higher was released, and as long as there was "no shading in the interpretation of facts."[116]

Attempts to have the Japanese manuscripts published continued. In Japan, members of the American Atomic Bomb Survey Group visited both Dr. Kelly of the Economic and Scientific Section of SCAP and the Public Health and Welfare Section. Kelly said that he, too, was eager to have the Japanese publish. The representative of the censors from PPB, who was also present, said that there was nothing one could do about publication in the United States, but when it came to Japan there were two processes that the manuscripts would have to go through: they must be checked by the Public Health and Welfare Section for medical accuracy and then by the Intelligence chief, G-2, because the material concerned atomic energy. As long as there was no "shading" of facts, there would be no objections from any section.[117]

But in February 1947 there was still uncertainty. There was no agreement within SCAP as to how Japanese manuscripts should be treated. On the one hand, lists of reports by Japanese scientists were to be sent to the Joint Chiefs of Staff with a request that they be checked for classification of technical information. Yet the Japanese Scientific Research Council, which received all Japanese reports on atomic bomb effects, had published a few documents in limited private editions. When this was reported to the Joint Chiefs there was consternation. In a handwritten note somebody warned that "this might become a 'Hot Potato.' " It was recommended that the whole matter be forwarded to the Atomic Energy Commission, and that SCAP be informed that no Japanese reports had been released for publication.[118] Shortly thereafter it was discovered that some Japanese reports had been published in the United States with portions deleted, others had not been cleared, but none had been cleared for publication in Japan. The procedure for seeking publication had been to refer all such material to Dr. Kelly of the Economic and Scientific Section, but evidently it was best to get dual clearance, from both the Atomic Energy Commission in the United States and Dr. Kelly at SCAP in Tokyo.[119]

At about this time one of the Americans investigating atomic bomb effects in Japan asked SCAP for permission at least to list Japanese as coauthors on reports. Two months later he still had no reply.[120] It was not that the request had disappeared into the bureaucracy; it was that SCAP still did not know what to do. In August a telegram was sent from SCAP to the Joint Chiefs of Staff requesting instructions. Which Japanese reports had been approved for publication in the United States? Could SCAP be kept informed of the status of Japanese reports in the future? The Joint

Chiefs promptly sent on the request to the Atomic Energy Commission.[121]

The AEC took more than three months to answer, and when the answer finally came, it pointed out that some of the Japanese reports were already declassified and had been widely distributed in the United States.[122] The Joint Chiefs then noted that there was a decision that reports on projects that had been cleared could also be published in Japan.[123] In January SCAP told the Joint Chiefs that the Japanese would be given permission to publish unless contrary advice was received before March.[124]

The Economic and Scientific Section, which initially had been regarded as having the authority to judge material on the atomic bomb, began to question the procedure. Now all material about Hiroshima and Nagasaki was referred to the Atomic Energy Commission in the United States, but could the AEC really decide on Japanese manuscripts and their publication in Japan? In other words, were Japanese considered to be under U.S. jurisdiction, which would mean that the Atomic Energy Act applied to them as well? The Legal Section of SCAP was of the opinion that the Atomic Energy Act was not applicable to non-U.S. citizens resident in Japan.[125] If the manuscripts could thus not be suppressed under the Atomic Energy Law, how could it then be done? Could SCAP, formally an overseer and guide for the Japanese government, make a law?[126] The problem does not seem to have been pursued.

In April, SCAP sent Dr. Kelly himself to the United States to visit the Atomic Energy Commission and get a final answer on publication policy regarding Japanese manuscripts.[127] But Dr. Kelly's trip was fruitless. He was informed that neither the Joint Chiefs of Staff, the Atomic Energy Commission, the Intelligence Section of the Department of the Army, nor the Army Institute of Pathology was ready to issue any instructions. They felt they were not fully informed about the situation in Japan and wanted a direct request from SCAP.[128]

It was June 1948 and SCAP was irritated. A radiogram was sent

to the Department of the Army restating the problem and emphasizing that for two years Japanese scientists had voluntarily submitted their manuscripts to SCAP, only to be told that they could
not publish even what had been released in the United States. In
the meantime it had become possible for less qualified scientists
to publish their work on the same subjects because of the introduction of postcensorship. This made the scientists feel they were
being penalized for cooperating with the Americans, and they
had stopped submitting new reports to SCAP. "To perform surveillance responsibility [over Japanese research] and to gather
technical information of interest to the United States it is essential that the goodwill of these Japanese scientists be recovered by
a definite policy," the radiogram warned. It also noted that there
were different opinions even within SCAP. The Intelligence Section, for example, still thought that it was undesirable to release
any manuscripts in Japan. The Joint Chiefs of Staff were thus
asked to make a decision.[129]

The radiogram also pointed out that it was impossible to keep
knowledge from the Japanese scientists. International mail
reached Japan, they possessed copies of their own papers and
could of course distribute those, and SCAP had made no attempt
to limit verbal discussions between scientists. In fact, classifying
these reports would only help foreign intelligence by emphasizing what the United States considered important. The United
States depended on the Japanese themselves to deny their information to other nations. To further emphasize the importance of
the matter, SCAP again sent an emissary to the AEC.[130]

The AEC finally realized that a decision had to be made. In
June it was suggested that a special board be set up to formulate a
policy. There was a feeling that perhaps only 20 percent of what
was classified needed to be so. This concerned not only "the
Japanese shots" but also the initial tests at Alamogordo and the
later ones at Bikini. The rest "could very well [be] declassified
entirely."[131]

In September the Joint Chiefs of Staff were informed of the

Figure 10. An Example of Mail Censorship

Source: SCAP, box 7431.

new policy. Documents dealing with the effects of the atomic bomb explosions in Japan could be published in cases where they were prepared by Japanese, if they had had no access to U.S. classified technical information and if they had had no collaboration involving classified technical information with Americans who had access to restricted data.[132] No special request would have to be made for a particular manuscript as long as it conformed to the policy. There was to be no special publicity about the new policy "since ill-informed people would conclude the Japanese were being allowed to engage in general research in the field of atomic energy in contradiction to the Far Eastern Commission policy on such matters."[133] The FEC, as noted above, had definitely rejected a U.S. suggestion that the Japanese be allowed to conduct certain kinds of research in the field of atomic energy. The question of freedom of speech was not an argument when publication of Japanese manuscripts was recommended. Neither did the recommendations emphasize the need for free medical discussion in order to help the atomic bomb survivors with their incurable diseases.

Finally, in January 1949, the first Japanese manuscripts on effects of the atomic bombings of Hiroshima and Nagasaki were declassified, including several that had been stamped Top Secret.[134] In the summer of that year the Japanese Special Committee for Investigation of Atomic Bomb Damage of the National Research Council was dissolved. This, according to a SCAP Activity Report, did not necessarily mean that Japanese scientists would completely abandon such research.[135] In fact, at the same time a laboratory was set up at the Atomic Bomb Casualty Commission (ABCC) as a joint U.S.-Japanese organization. The ABCC did research in Hiroshima and Nagasaki on the effects of radiation on human beings. There was much bitterness among the survivors that the ABCC did not offer any treatment, and they often said that they felt like guinea pigs in relation to the ABCC.

For the most part, both Japanese and American official research ignored the need for treatment of survivors. According to

Yukuo Sasamoto, a Japanese researcher, there are no records of the Japanese Army issuing any order to help the survivors immediately after the bombings, although it did send several survey groups to the bombed cities. Although there was extensive and detailed Japanese research, there was no plan to help the survivors later either.[136] With the exception of Red Cross relief, sent on order from MacArthur in September 1945, little or nothing was done to help the atomic bomb victims. The Japanese government made no surveys in order to assist them. Because of the destruction, it is unclear how long the government sent disaster relief to the cities. According to remaining records, general relief seems to have been provided for only two months in both Hiroshima and Nagasaki, because that was all the Wartime Casualties Law provided for. The atomic bomb victims had to pay their own medical expenses after that. There were no funds for rebuilding hospitals. A reconstruction plan for Hiroshima was announced in November 1946, but there were no government measures to aid the atomic bomb victims. When the peace treaty with the United States was signed in 1951, Japan relinquished all rights to press claims on the United States, and this was later interpreted by the Japanese government as including any claims made by atomic bomb victims.[137] Sasamoto expressly accuses the Japanese government of cooperating with the United States in surveying the damage, not for the sake of the victims, but in an attempt to win goodwill and achieve better relations. The Japanese government cooperated in researching the results of the aggression while ignoring the victims. This, Sasamoto concludes, makes the Japanese government too an aggressor against the survivors.[138]

REASONS FOR CENSORING
THE ATOMIC BOMB

As the preceding pages have shown, there were many reasons why the United States suppressed publication in Japan of material about the atomic bombings of Hiroshima and Nagasaki. The security of the United States, which, it was said, demanded secrecy about the bomb, was one. Fear of criticism of the United States by Japanese was another. The campaign of impressing war guilt on the Japanese was also involved. But above all there was concern about the reputation of the United States. An often-stated reason for suppression was that the material gave the impression that the United States was inhumane or barbaric in using the atomic bomb.

The question of security had been of great importance from the start of the atomic bomb project. The bomb was developed with Great Britain as a junior partner, but the third great ally of the United States, the Soviet Union, was not even told of its existence. At Potsdam in July 1945 when President Truman mentioned to Stalin that the United States had a new weapon, he explained nothing about the nature of that weapon. Stalin showed little interest. There is a debate among historians as to whether he did not understand the importance of what Truman said or, on the contrary, whether he knew only too well what Truman meant, because Soviet spies had long been involved with the projects.

After the war ended, a debate ensued in the United States over the extent to which information about the atomic bomb should be made available to the rest of the world. The opinion prevailed that maximum secrecy should be maintained. It was acknowledged, however, that the United States would not be able to keep its nuclear monopoly forever, and moves were made to arrange, under the auspices of the United Nations, for an international control organ for atomic energy. The United States officially supported these efforts. At the same time, while conventional military forces were reduced, there was a policy of reliance on the relatively cheap atomic weapon, trusting that the United States would remain the only nuclear power for some time.

Even when it was realized that this exclusive ownership could only last a few years, at most, secrecy was advocated for the momentary advantage it gave. As Edwin Teller, the "father of the hydrogen bomb," put it, "For a few short years after the end of World War II, justification for our continued nuclear secrecy seemed substantial. We had an atomic monopoly and in our arrogance we believed that the scientists of other nations would require decades to rediscover our atomic secrets. . . . Secrecy it was thought, could perform a high service: It could provide security."[1]

The Joint Strategic Survey Committee, in more terse sentences, said that the United States should "make every possible effort to maintain this advantage [the atomic bomb monopoly], and to advance more rapidly in scientific warfare than any other nation. To this end it should be our firm policy to provide for . . . maintenance of the highest possible degree of secrecy with respect to the atomic bomb and refusal to give these secrets to any other nation or to the United Nations organization."[2]

As for Japanese atomic bomb material, the possibility that it might contain something detrimental to the security of the United States often lead to protracted checking between different agencies, both within SCAP and within departments and agencies in the United States. A decision on whether such material could be published could take several years, as was the case with the manuscripts of Japanese scientists who had investigated the effects of the bombings. There was, however, a certain confusion as to why Japanese manuscripts should be suppressed. Sometimes, it seemed, they were checked from a purely scientific viewpoint or for "technical accuracy." At other times, the security of the United States was the paramount consideration.

The very first case of material suppressed because of references to the atomic bombings was that of Domei in September 1945. The news agency was closed down for twenty-four hours for having written that Japan might not have lost the war if it had not been for the atomic bomb, and that the atomic bombings were barbaric acts. Two forbidden statements were the prime offenders: one gave an explanation for the war's end that was contrary to the American version and showed not a trace of "war guilt" on the Japanese part, and the second was a judgment on the United States for having used the atomic bombs.

A third reason given for suppressing nonscientific material about the atomic bombings was that it might cause resentment of the United States.

One of the stated purposes of the Occupation was to demilitarize Japan. To do this, the Civil Information and Education Section of SCAP undertook special campaigns, during which the Japanese were informed about atrocities that their military had committed during the war. These campaigns included material for publication or broadcast. In addition, many school books, especially in subjects like history, which had been used for militaristic propaganda, were banned for a long period, in some subjects more than a year. Only gradually were they replaced by new ones. Blacklisted books of all kinds were collected from bookshops by special American teams. These books included classical Japanese works that were deemed to contain "emperor worship."[3] The work got underway early in the Occupation. At the beginning of October 1945 a SCAP report noted that there was "little consciousness of war guilt when the occupation forces entered Tokyo. . . . there was widespread belief that Japan's defeat was due solely to industrial and scientific inferiority and to the atomic bomb.''[4]

To the Americans, the Domei statement that Japan would not have lost the war had it not been for the atomic bomb must have seemed proof that the Japanese saw their defeat as being caused by something other than their own shortcomings or, as the war guilt campaigns tried to instill, their evil, inhuman acts. (Curiously enough, forty-five years after the end of the war, many Americans and others continue to believe that Japan surrendered only because of the atomic bombings. Some justify the American use the atomic bomb as necessary to save the lives of a great number of American soldiers, varying from a few hundred thousand to one million.)

''Lack of war guilt'' could also be expressed in a sentence like ''many innocent people were killed in Hiroshima and Nagasaki.''[5] This was deleted, and one can only suppose that it was because, in the eyes of the censors, Japanese should not be allowed to feel they were innocent and that the atomic bomb was used for no reason. Even young Masako Ishida mentioned that defeat made her feel mortified.[6] In her case, though, the censor did not pay special attention to what could possibly be labeled as lack of war guilt. Instead, he pointed out that her book as a whole might bring resentment against the United States.

The question of how the Japanese would react toward the Americans was one of the most worrisome and incalculable factors when it became clear that Japan would surrender. It had been taken for granted that if the planned invasion had taken place, it would have been followed by heavy, protracted fighting like that during the invasion of Okinawa in the spring of 1945. It was expected that resistance on the so-called home islands would be even greater. But there was no fighting, just a landing. How would the Americans be received? With hatred or with submissiveness? Most, although not General MacArthur, thought with hatred. The war had been fierce, the Japanese were pictured as fanatics, and now their country would be occupied for the first time in history. Since March, the United States had firebombed their cities to ruins, burning down practically all of Tokyo and most other cities too. In addition, they had destroyed Hiroshima and Nagasaki with atomic bombs. Minister of War Henry Stimson, who had thought much about the possible effects of the atomic bomb, wrote in his diary that he feared that the "bitterness which would be caused by such a wanton act [as the pondered atomic bombing of the old capital Kyoto] might make it impossible during the long postwar period to reconcile the Japanese to us in that area rather than to the Russians."[7]

To have the Japanese think too much about what had happened at Hiroshima and Nagasaki would possibly lead to resentment of the United States. When Dr. Nagai wrote about the horrors of Nagasaki with its destroyed medical equipment and dead medical personnel, the censors thought that such a book would be a constant reminder of what the Japanese had suffered at the hand of the Allies. Now or in the future, such a book might raise anti-American feelings.

In addition to these reasons, the censors and censoring agencies also suppressed material because it was said to give the impression that the Americans had been inhumane in using the atomic bomb.

The moral question of whether to use the bomb or not was a basic question wrestled with at all levels as the bomb was being developed. There was never any consensus among Americans regarding its use, once it became clear that it would not be ready in time to use against Germany but would be used against Japan. Politicians, scientists, and the military expressed their opposition to a weapon that had such terrible effects. Admiral William Leahy, chief of staff to presidents Roosevelt and Truman, wrote:

> My own feeling was that in being the first to use it, we had adopted an ethical standard common to the barbarians of the Dark Ages. . . . [Using the atomic bomb] would take us back in cruelty toward noncombatants to the days of Genghis Khan. It will be a form of pillage and rape of a society done impersonally by one state

against another whereas in the Dark Ages it was a result of individual greed and vandalism. These new and terrible instruments of uncivilized warfare represent a modern type of barbarism not worthy of Christian man.[8]

Secretary of War Stimson, who had said that "the reputation of the United States for fair play and humanitarianism is the world's biggest asset for peace in the coming decades," wrote that the atomic bomb raised issues that "went right down to the bottom facts of human nature, morals and government."[9] He had already been concerned during the fire bombings of Japanese cities: "I did not want to have the United States get the reputation for outdoing Hitler in atrocities."[10]

Undersecretary of the Navy Ralph Bard advocated that Japan be warned before it was atom bombed, giving as his reason that the United States occupied a position as a great humanitarian nation with a fair-play attitude.[11]

The scientists who had developed the bomb were also concerned about the moral aspects of using it. Edward Teller writes that most of the Los Alamos scientists were "profoundly disturbed by the questionable morality of using the atomic bomb without first warning the Japanese. After Nagasaki, the moral doubts deepened."[12] In a special report, the so-called Franck Report, several of the scientists voiced a deep concern and warned that if the United States used the atomic bomb, "this new means of indiscriminate destruction," public support throughout the world would be sacrificed. The report talked about loss of confidence in the United States and the wave of horror and repulsion that would sweep the world.[13]

Albert Einstein wrote to President Roosevelt that any military advantages of nuclear weapons would be offset by the political and psychological damage to American prestige.[14]

According to President Truman, on his part the decision to use the atomic bomb was taken without any second thoughts.[15] But others continued to be concerned about the moral effects. In the spring of 1945 Stimson wrote that "certain things . . . must be done . . . to avoid the risk of grave repercussions on the public in general and on Congress in particular." By this he meant that arrangements must be made for special, "appropriate" publicity about the atomic bomb.[16]

The Japanese, on the other hand, had no interest in protecting the reputation of the United States. On August 11, 1945, in a dispatch through the Swiss Embassy, which represented Japan, the Japanese government formally protested against the atomic bombings and declared them a crime against international law.[17] Radio Tokyo sent out detailed reports describing Hiroshima as a city of death, where sufferers pleaded to be killed. Domei sent overseas dispatches telling how reconstruction workers became ill and how the toll of dead mounted weeks after the bombing. This included special propaganda programs intended for American soldiers. In one such program from Radio Tokyo, two persons named John and Sam discussed "A New Weapon." They tried to refute American charges of Japanese atrocities by belittling them, saying they were difficult to prove and, not the least, comparing them to the atomic bomb.

> Sam: Oh, I guess that [the atomic bomb] will make our reputation go up like a . . . we have already killed thousands of innocent civilians with them.
> John: Say, how come you're talking as though you don't want to win this war?
> Sam: I want to be fair. I want to win the war as much as you do, but slaughtering innocent civilians isn't my idea of winning a victory. It's against our principles, constitution, in fact it's against the principles of humanity.
> John: Everything is fair in love and war, Sam, and if the atom bombs will bring us a quick victory, why not?
> Sam: Oh, I don't think that victory means just hitting below the belt or stabbing a man in the back—real victory.[18]

However justified the Japanese protests against the atomic bombings seem to be, they were of the same type made by the government for propaganda purposes. Above all, they did not seem to reflect genuine concern for atomic bomb survivors, even less for the future of the world. The Japanese researcher Yukuo Sasamoto accuses both the Japanese and the Americans of using the atomic bombings in an information and propaganda war. The Japanese government, according to his analysis, moved between appeasing the victorious United States, on the one hand, and exploiting the facts about the effects of the bombings to squeeze out better surrender conditions for itself, on the other. For appeasement, the Japanese government did not use the word "atomic bomb" in the official protest, something Sasamoto sees as lenient toward the United States. In any case, it did not help the survivors or defend their human rights. He also sees Japanese cooperation in surveys of atomic bomb damage as only helping the United States in its weapon and defense needs. The results were not used for alleviating illnesses and improving material conditions for the survivors. Sasamoto sees the widespread Japanese dissemination of information about the horrible effects in Hiroshima and Nagasaki, and the accusations that the United States broke international law by using the atomic bomb, as only a government attempt immediately after the bombings to create a bargaining chip, never made with the intention of supporting the cause of the survivors.[19]

The reaction of the U.S. administration to the Japanese accusations was to call them propaganda. Even the official Japanese protest against the atomic bombing of Hiroshima was referred only to experts on Japanese propaganda, and they were of the opinion that the Japanese might be trying to "capitalize on the horror of the atomic bombing in an effort to win sympathy from their conquerors." By bringing out allegations "offensive to American humanitarianism," they might be "trying to shorten the occupation and lessen reparations."[20]

Through the listening post of Magic, which had broken the code of the Japanese foreign ministry, the American government could follow communications between Tokyo and Japanese embassies abroad right until the end of their operation in the middle of September 1945. The Japanese ambassador in Lisbon, Morishima, thought that when it came to the question of war crimes, Japan could expose the United States, since the use of the atomic bomb "inescapably" must be regarded as a crime against humanity. No distinction should be made between victors and vanquished before the law.[21] Three days later, on September 13, Foreign Minister Mamoru Shigemitsu sent a report to the Japanese legations in Sweden, Switzerland, and Portugal informing them about Japanese newspaper reports from Hiroshima and Nagasaki. It was also pointed out that Domei had broadcast the full details abroad. The foreign minister now wanted to know to what extent Domei's reports had been carried by news media in those countries. According to Shigemitsu, the United States had been "raising an uproar" about Japanese mistreatment of prisoners. He thought that Japan "should make every effort to exploit the atomic bomb question in our propaganda." He wanted advice from the Japanese legations abroad on whether this would be desirable.[22]

The Japanese ambassadors in Stockholm and Berne urged Tokyo to avoid creating an impression that it was conducting a propaganda campaign. But the ambassador to Sweden, Okamoto, had another idea that might allow Japan to accomplish the same goals "unobtrusively." He suggested that announcements should be made for home consumption only, but then be carried by British and Americans news agencies abroad. English and American journalists should also be made to write stories about atomic bomb damage. In this way the world would get a "powerful impression."[23] At least one independent reporter, the Australian Wilfred Burchett, was accused by the American military of exactly that—falling prey to Japanese propaganda—when he wrote about the conditions he had personally observed in Hiroshima.

The Japanese ambassador in Portugal reported that the Japanese accounts of the atomic bombs were carried in Portuguese media, but that the reports about Japanese atrocities had overshadowed them. He suggested that the Apostolic Nuncio in Japan be furnished with facts. That "might be rather effective," the ambassador thought.[24]

There the Magic summaries stop, for the simple reason that communication between the Foreign Ministry and its legations ended. The Occupation authorities had taken over control. Already almost a week earlier Domei had had to stop its transmissions abroad. It was no longer possible for the Japanese government to influence the reporting about Hiroshima and Nagasaki. Neither were there many possibilities for the survivors in Hiroshima and Nagasaki to tell their version of the atomic bombings.

For the American Occupation authorities, the risk that the United States would be regarded as barbaric and inhumane remained in their minds. Sometimes they tried to balance accounts that gave such an impression by accounts of Japanese atrocities, as reasoned in the case of Dr. Nagai. The United States was not to be accused; guilt was only for Japan, for its barbarous acts in the war, as General Willoughby categorically explained. As has been shown above, this was a view that permeated the whole Occupation policy.

The censorship of material about Hiroshima and Nagasaki reflected American concerns not only about the security of the United States and of its Occupation troops but also about the moral implications of using nuclear weapons. The concerns did not originate in Japanese propaganda or even among the atomic bomb victims. They had already for some time been aired among American politicians, military, and scientists involved with the manufacture and use of the atomic bomb.

10

RESULTS OF U.S. CENSORSHIP OPERATIONS IN JAPAN

DURING its planning for the postwar occupation of Japan, the United States set up the basis for censorship operations. These were regarded as a normal military undertaking in the occupation of any enemy territory. But gradually the concept changed. It became clear that Japan, in contrast to Germany, was not going to be led by a military government run by the Occupation forces. The Japanese government and Japanese institutions were to be preserved, albeit mostly under new leadership. But their policy was to be shaped by the Supreme Commander of the Allied Powers. The Occupation troops would oversee the execution of these policies. That the line between shaping policies and executing them often became very diffuse is well known. The most famous example is the writing of the new constitution, which in reality was presented by SCAP to the Japanese government for acceptance.

Because Japan had never in its long history experienced an occupation and because the war had been so bitter, the Japanese government was at a loss as to how to prepare for the arrival of the Occupation troops. Japan's future was uncertain, and people feared the worst. In the interval between the surrender declaration and the arrival of American troops, a period of about two weeks, the government made its preparations. The aim was naturally to retain as much as possible of the old structure while cooperating with the occupiers. The suspicion on both sides was,

understandably, great. Journalist Mark Gayn, who was critical of
SCAP but also suspicious of the Japanese, was probably right
when he wrote:

> Japan did not surrender blindly. As soon as her rulers decided to
> give in, they put Japan's entire, closely knit, efficient machinery of
> government to the job of circumventing the pledges they were utter-
> ing to the victors. They made good use of the two-week interval
> between the announcement of their surrender and the arrival of the
> first American units. Documents were burned. Government funds
> were dispersed where they would do the most good. Stocks of valu-
> able material were concealed. Detailed plans were made for keeping
> the government apparatus intact whatever the conqueror's orders.[1]

The differences of opinion among departments of SCAP were
numerous, both on general policy questions and on individual
cases, as shown in the area of censorship. In addition, the con-
flicts among different departments within the administration in
Washington influenced the implementation of policies in Japan.[2]
Because SCAP was only introducing and overseeing policies that
should be implemented by Japanese institutions, there were inev-
itably not only clashes but also alliances between Americans and
Japanese:

> Although formal power lay unquestionably in the hands of the
> Americans, the Occupation rarely, if ever, involved a united Ameri-
> can occupier attempting to reform a united (and presumably op-
> posed) body of Japanese. Familiarity, constant contact, and the
> emergence of compatible goals between particular groups of Japa-
> nese and Americans led rather to a large number of functional and
> organizational alliances that crossed national lines.[3]

These points have to be taken into account when evaluating
the results of the censorship operations. In contrast to most other
areas, SCAP had executive power regarding censorship. But the
very concept of censorship changed several times during the Occupation. Censorship was transformed from a routine military

undertaking to a much larger, more complicated operation. Originally, censorship was used primarily to collect intelligence, maintain security, discover attempts to violate military order, and the like. But the aim of the Occupation was, in the words of the Freedom and Speech Directive issued by SCAP on September 10, 1945, for Japan to "emerge from defeat as a new nation entitled to a place among the peace-loving nations of the world." In this endeavor, censorship would be an essential tool. Through censorship, militarism and reverence for the emperor would be uprooted and replaced by democratic ideals. Censorship should also "assist in the free and factual dissemination of news." The American pronouncements envisaged a Japan where everybody had free access to information and news of the world, where everybody could say and write what they wanted, where there was no censorship. These were, as Supreme Commander Douglas MacArthur said, freedoms for which the Allies had fought the war.

There was, however, yet another side to the Occupation and the censorship operations. Here the aim was to draw a ring around Japan through which no unauthorized information slipped, either to or from Japan. Seen from this angle, Japan was a territory separated both from most of the world, including to a large extent the allies of the United States. It was to be remade in the image of the Americans. It was also to be separated from its own past, and from developments of the world, until the transformation was accomplished.

In this version of the Occupation, Japanese could not communicate with the outside world. Not only was there a ban on travel and censorship of private mail, but the ability of the Japanese to inform the world of what was happening in their own country was also cut off. From September 1945, when the news agency Domei was prohibited to transmit overseas, any information about conditions in Japan would have to come from American sources or the few visitors to Japan who were approved by SCAP.

All incoming correspondence and information, including

American, was also screened by Occupation censors. It was forbidden entry if judged inimical to the goals of the Occupation. Under such rules, not even criticism of the Occupation voiced outside Japan was allowed into the country.

Under this system, the Japanese had limited sources for knowledge about the world. Instead of having "free access to news sources of the world," they were not allowed to know about many aspects of both world and national affairs.

The world was also limited in its knowledge of Japan under the American Occupation. Every foreign journalist who wanted to visit or work in Japan had to be accredited by the Occupation authorities. Those journalists were, to a large extent, Americans. In May 1946 there were seventy Allied correspondents in Japan, of whom only fourteen were non-Americans. Not even the largest and most influential British media had their own correspondents. They relied instead on reports from American news agencies or reporters, who occasionally sent them stories.[4]

Visitors often found it hard to work freely: "The Public Relations Section [of SCAP] took pains to arrange that visitors to Japan, particularly if they were publicists, should be properly 'orientated.' Every precaution was taken to protect these visitors from coming in contact with any of the unpleasant facts of life," wrote the Commonwealth representative on the Allied Council, MacMahon Ball.[5]

Those who reported critically on the Occupation have often told about the strained relations with SCAP that this caused, including obstruction and nonrenewal of work permits. The correspondents were dissatisfied almost from the beginning. Accredited to the fighting forces, they were still under military censorship. But until Occupation censorship was set up, the Japanese media were relatively free. Domei, for example, at first could transmit news freely to the world. The Allied correspondents complained to SCAP: "We are being made the laughingstock of the world for getting beaten on our own news."[6] Not until October 6, 1945, was censorship for foreign correspondents in Japan lifted.[7] But the clashes between GHQ and the foreign journalists continued. Several journalists were expelled, the most famous case being that of Mark Gayn, who had reported on a secret conference at GHQ regarding a purge of Japanese business executives. Gayn refused to name his source. After that, the correspondents were informed: "SCAP officers could declare as classified any material they wanted to. He [Brigadier General Frayne Baker, MacArthur's public relations officer] also pointed out that newsmen could be courtmartialed under the Articles of War for publishing such information since the United States and Japan technically were still at war."[8]

In 1948, the correspondents were still so frustrated that they wrote a report to the chairman of the Committee on Freedom of the Press of the American Society of Newspaper Editors, naming several cases of how they were obstructed by SCAP. Among them were SCAP officials using military security as a pretext for seeking the expulsion from Japan of correspondents who had written stories considered critical of the Occupation. They had also tried for eighteen months to get a clear definition of peacetime security, with no success. "Every effort was made to remove offending correspondents if the pressures in Tokyo failed to bring them into line," wrote Ball.[9]

The American remaking of Japan was not exclusively motivated by a hatred for militarism. That became clear during the course of the Occupation. Censorship policies are revealing in this regard. At first they were expressly aimed at, among other things, shielding all the Allies from criticism. But during later years, criticism of the Soviet Union was exempted. This change coincided with a seemingly complete reorientation of the policies of the Occupation from demilitarization and democratization, where all political views left of extreme right were encouraged, to one of "red purge," where leftists were banned not only from government positions and teaching, but also from private businesses, such as publishing.

There is evidence suggesting that prior to the war the United

States had targeted Japan as a potential ally in the struggle for world influence, and that the war was only an interim, however regrettable, obstacle to this long-range plan.[10] Such a concept does not seem to have been completely alien to the Soviet leaders. In meetings with Stalin, American Ambassador to the Soviet Union Averell Harriman was not seriously rebuffed even when he stated that the United States would not allow the Soviet Union to be a part of the Occupation by stationing troops on the northernmost island of Hokkaido.

Seeing how important the remaking of Japan was to the United States and what an essential part censorship had in this undertaking, it is amazing to study the workings of censorship operations in practice. It becomes abundantly clear that American censorship was deficient in terms of effectiveness and consistency. There was a kind of thoughtlessness about it from the very beginning. The planners regarded it as a routine military operation to control an enemy but completely ignored important sources of information. It took the director of the Office of Censorship to point out that radio, press, and other mass media ought to be included.

There was also a serious lack of practical planning, to the extent that it came as a surprise that there were so few Japanese-speaking personnel. When this was realized, people of many different nationalities were used, for the sole reason that they had language ability. Knowing both Japanese and English hardly ensured either ability as a censor in a professional sense or adherence to American ideals.

But what were the American ideals? The most basic criticism of the censorship, from the point of effectiveness, was that there was no consistency in ideals. Guidelines changed often, and it was seldom clear to the censors why. For instance, at one time nothing negative could be said about the Soviet Union, but at another time anything might be allowed.

There was also nervousness on the part of the Occupation authorities about the fact that censorship existed at all. It did not fit in with the official American ideals of freedom. Censorship was un-American. Some suggested that it should at least be called something else. Others tried to convince foreign correspondents in particular that it had to exist. In several cases, censorship action was avoided out of deference to how foreign correspondents might react.

The difficulties with censorship made many Occupation officials wonder if it was really worth the trouble. In 1946, some within SCAP advocated that it should be scrapped. When it finally was discarded in 1949, the reason given officially was that Japan had become sufficiently democratic.

Japan knew what was expected of it. Punishment for censorship violations existed, from confiscation to years at hard labor, although it was never publicized. But punishment had never been the main means for the Americans to extend their control. Censorship ruled more by warnings and suggestions. Before the Occupation, an editor could be punished with years in prison, even death. Censorship was all-pervading during the war. The Japanese were used to it and practiced some degree of self-censorship as a precaution. It was not difficult to continue this way of thinking and reacting when the Americans came. But the Americans also controlled the Japanese media by appeals to democracy, in ways similar to what had been done in the United States during the war. The Japanese constantly were told that they should feel guilt for their behavior during the war, and that the alternative to their wicked ideals was democracy, the American way. The Japanese were not sure what the Americans meant by this. In censorship as in many other areas, Japanese and Americans often did not understand each other, even when they used the same words. Undoubtedly, most Japanese became convinced that democracy was better than militarism. Even if they were not convinced, or if they wanted to question the American way, they were used to being careful in their relations with authorities and avoiding controversy. Since they were used to censorship, they were perhaps not so upset with the American version. Perhaps they compared their situation not with the ideal of democracy but with the society they had lived in before the Occupation. In addition, they were only furnished with the American interpretation of democracy. They were told that they could publish what was good from a democratic point of view. If it was not good, it was censored. By definition, then, censored writing was an example of undemocratic, or at least anti-Occupation, thinking.

Furthermore, few persons knew that censorship existed. The only ones aware of it were those directly in contact with the censors, that is, writers, editors, and journalists. They were not allowed to publish even the fact that there was censorship. Its existence was secret.

American censorship in Japan was erratic. It was often irritating to the individual censors, who were ignorant of their undertaking and sometimes also of the country in which they were working. It was costly. Not the least, it was contrary to the ideals of democracy. Far from being used only to protect Allied troops and to root out militarism, censorship was used to control and sift information, and thus stifle discussion on many subjects of concern to people everywhere. In spite of its shortcomings, however, it was quite effective. One example was the extent to which it managed to control knowledge and discussion about the effects and consequences of the atomic bomb.

Censorship of the Atomic Bomb

Nowhere in its censorship operations was the discrepancy between the needs and goals of the United States and its ideals more evident than in the case of the atomic bomb. Censorship was purportedly introduced to make Japan democratic. But did publication of material about conditions in the bombed cities of Hiroshima and Nagasaki in any way harm the development of democracy in Japan?

The different points of the Press Code, which was used as a yardstick for what could be published in Japan during the Occupation, could be justified as intended to further democracy and protect the Occupation troops. Censorship of the reports about the atomic bomb was different, however. These reports had no direct relation to any of the rules in the Press Code. When they were censored, often the most elastic of rules was used: that of disturbing public tranquility. This is a rule used by censors the world over to justify censorship of items that cannot be justified in any other way; in Japan, it was used to protect exclusively American interests, unrelated to the demilitarization and democratization of Japan.

As in the case of Occupation censorship in general, censorship of the atomic bomb was erratic. The atomic bomb was the victim not only of the vicissitudes of American censorship in general, but also of widely conflicting views within the American administration, society, and GHQ.

As the Occupation of Japan started, the atmosphere was military. Japan was a defeated enemy that must be subdued. The Japanese should be taught their place in the world: as a defeated nation, Japan had no status and was entitled to no respect. People should be made to realize that any catastrophe that had befallen them was of their own making. Until they had repented, they were suspect. If they wanted to release information about the atomic bombings of Hiroshima and Nagasaki, it could only be for the wrong reasons, such as accusing the United States of inhumanity. Thus this information was suppressed.

But even the sternest military men sometimes changed their minds on the question of publication. They did it not because their impression of the Japanese had changed, but because a release might be better for the United States. The world was not closed, like Japan. Facts about the atomic bombs were known. Let the Japanese know too. If there was Japanese resentment or even enmity, one line of reasoning went, it would be better to let it out into the open, while it was still possible for SCAP to influence the results, to defend America with force or arguments.

Whether the dropping of the atomic bombs could effectively be defended or not was a question of concern to some Americans. In the world just after the war, the United States was widely regarded as the great savior from Nazism and fascism and the horrors they had brought. The wastelands of Hiroshima and Nagasaki were not consistent with this image of a humanitarian, altruistic America. Accusations that the United States had also broken international law by using a weapon worse than bacteria and gas could not be tolerated, especially not from an enemy as cruel as Japan. Under the Occupation, the cruelty of the atomic bomb was occasionally justified as a means to end the cruelty of the Japanese. But more often such accusations were prohibited completely.

In a political and somewhat wider military sense, however, Japan soon was no longer regarded as an enemy. Instead, it was being groomed to become an ally. In light of this development, one discussion about Hiroshima and Nagasaki among Occupation authorities centered on the possibly positive results of publication of details about the bombings. It might serve to show the horrors of war. It might also underline that Japan was now a trusted collaborator, with whom the frightening results of the new weapon were researched, so that this weapon would never be used again.

American scientists in government service who were trying to gauge the impact of the atomic bombs on human beings and the environment were some of those who pleaded for release of information about bomb research in Japan. Publication would be an encouragement for Japanese scientists to continue follow-up studies in Hiroshima and Nagasaki. The United States needed the Japanese scientists in order to find the results. They could do the necessary research for the nuclear development and civil defense of the United States, not only now but for decades to come. Hiroshima and Nagasaki were, after all, unique testing grounds for the new weapon.

From an American point of view, a great risk with the release of facts about conditions in Hiroshima and Nagasaki was that public tranquility might be deeply disturbed. Resentment against the United States and the Occupation troops was only one facet; another, and perhaps more important, was the anguish that many would feel if they knew not only of the immediate injuries caused by the atomic bomb, but also of the future effects.

To the Manhattan Engineering District and the Atomic Energy Commission, all facts about atomic bombs were "from birth" secret. But this view was by no means unanimous among those directly concerned with the decision of how to treat information about the bomb. In August 1945, one of the leading scientists on the atomic bomb project, Arthur Compton, wrote a memorandum about the scientists' opinions. He suggested that those who had technical knowledge should be allowed to express views on the political and social problems involved with the use of the bomb. Furthermore, all scientific information about the design and effectiveness of the weapon should be published. "The world should know the potential destructiveness of the new weapon in order to consider the cost of another war," Compton wrote after the attack on Hiroshima.[11]

Another scientist, Edward Teller, who was obsessed by the thought of building a bigger, better bomb—the hydrogen bomb—was upset about secrecy for another reason. Many years later, he recalled a postwar conference with the military. He claimed they had no knowledge of the real implications, technical or political, of the atomic bomb. He blamed secrecy for the situation.

> With secrecy preventing discussion of all new facts, it was only natural that the military men should accept, in our bizarre atomic world, only those changes that they had to accept. The "bomb" was an unassailable fact, and had to be accepted. But there was no opportunity, because of secrecy, and no incentive, because of inertia, to think further ahead. I am firmly convinced that in the early postwar years secrecy was a powerful barrier between military men who were clinging to the past and scientists who were turning away from what seemed a frightening future.[12]

Even the Smyth Report, which was the official report on the atomic bomb project, stated: "Because of the restrictions of military security there has been no chance for the Congress or the people to debate such questions [as the implications for all of mankind of the atomic bomb]. In a free country like ours, such questions should be debated by the people and decisions must be made by the people through their representatives.''[13]

But the Joint Chiefs of Staff decided that free information about the atomic bomb would accelerate the arms race, make the United States vulnerable to atomic bomb attacks, hinder international control of atomic power, and, not the least, be a sign of weakness. In their discussions, they talked openly of keeping the knowledge expressly from the Soviet Union. Only a sense of diplomacy, or strategy, kept them from naming the Soviet Union openly in their recommendation to the president. But they were unanimous in their opinion that only the most cursory facts pertaining to atomic bombs would be given away.

In spite of this, the secret, of course, was out. The Soviet Union got its own bomb; scientists in several countries made their own rediscoveries, sometimes helped by spies. Soon keeping secrets that were no secrets became only cumbersome. The Atomic Energy Commission started declassifying material. Sometimes this material had already been published, even in the United States. Last of all, the Japanese were allowed to know what the rest of the world already knew, what they themselves lived with.

There was no coordination of the differing views about release of information about the atomic bombings of Hiroshima and Nagasaki. Local Occupation policy depended on persons as far apart as lower-echelon censors and SCAP himself. And although MacArthur seemed to have power to say the final word in censorship questions as long as he did not intend to abolish censorship altogether, he deferred to Washington important cases. He was encouraged to do so by the Joint Chiefs of Staff, on the basis of national security.

When a request for a decision on publication of atomic bomb material did come to Washington from Japan, it caused confusion, postponements, and inaction. One would think the answers would have been simple to find in an atmosphere where the cold war already dominated international politics. But it was as if Japan did not fit into any larger pattern. Requests for decisions about censorship of atomic bomb material in Japan brought confusion and referral of decisions to all kinds of departments.

Atomic bomb censorship in Japan produced a gap between what the Japanese knew about the atomic bomb and what the world knew. The Japanese were well aware of the initial horrors from the days between the surrender and the occupation in August and September 1945. Newspapers and radio broadcasts reported extensively from the ruined cities. With the Occupation, news coverage became scant and erratic. Released news was sometimes good news, claiming that all the survivors were now well. Japanese also heard that in Hiroshima and Nagasaki some survivors, asking why the atomic bomb had struck them, answered that it was fate or an act of God. That was about all that was allowed in Japan.

The rest of the world had also heard the first reports beamed abroad. They had read about the reactions of the American fliers who saw the cities destroyed and were shocked. They had also read the detailed interviews from Hiroshima by the American journalist John Hersey. They had listened to scientists speculating on the effects, and sometimes even publishing results of research. Above all, they had been able to follow and participate in the debate on what this weapon meant, both for the United States and for the world.

But all—Japanese, Americans, everyone—had been limited to random pieces of information. Scattered facts about the atomic bomb appeared. Some voices were heard from Hiroshima and Nagasaki. But there was no order, no full picture. A full picture is difficult to form of anything, but regarding the atomic bomb, there was one aspect concerning which a reasonably accurate picture could have been made but was not, because of American censorship. This was the after-effects of the atomic bombings of Hiroshima and Nagasaki. "The atomic bomb sickness," took many lives in the period right after the bombings. To this day, the survivors fall ill and die from these effects. Even those who do not fall ill have to live with the fear of falling ill. Worse, they live with the fear that their children will inherit some incurable illness. In spite of research seemingly showing that there is no hereditary risk, there are no absolute proofs. Above all, there is continuing fear. The ignorance about the bomb bred discrimination, poverty, and loneliness for many survivors. Knowledge and discussion of these effects would not only have been information on which to base opinions about the atomic bomb, but a concrete basis on which doctors who tried to treat the survivors of Hiroshima and Nagasaki could have worked. They could have helped to alleviate the physical, psychological, and social pains of the survivors and their families. But the hundreds of reports and studies that were made disappeared into American archives, stamped Top Secret. As it was, there were only random facts mixed with speculation.

The end result of the U.S. censorship of the atomic bombings of Hiroshima and Nagasaki was that for years the world did not know the full extent of what happens when nuclear weapons are used. It was well known that the atomic bomb caused terrible physical destruction, and that many people died instantly. It was also understood that the world had changed because of this new weapon. The balance of power had changed with the power of destruction. But the implications for human beings were hidden. Censorship not only deleted certain facts, it hindered atomic bomb survivors from speaking out about their experiences, experiences that they alone had had and that would have helped the rest of mankind understand what the world had come to. They could not or would not speak, out of deference to the Americans, out of fear, or because they did not want trouble. Through censorship, Japan was closed to the world. The facts that did seep out about Hiroshima and Nagasaki in all likelihood had less impact than the same facts would have had multiplied through the eyes and pens and voices of many reporters.

One is hard put not to agree with the Japanese historian Seiji Imahori, who said that by silencing the voice of the atomic bomb survivors "an important possibility to decisively influence the world situation was lost."[14]

NOTES

Abbreviations for Record Groups

AS	Records of Army Staff, RG 319
JCS	Records of Joint Chiefs of Staff, RG 218
Magic	Records of the National Security Agency, Magic Diplomatic Summaries, RG 457
MED	Records of Manhattan Engineering District, Records of the Office of the Chief of Engineers, RG 77
SCAP	Records of Allied Operational and Occupational Headquarters, World War II (Supreme Commander of the Allied Powers), RG 331
SD	Records of the Department of State, RG 51
SD/FS	Records of the Department of State, Foreign Service Posts, RG 84
USSBS	Records of United States Strategic Bombing Survey, RG 243
WD	Records of the Department of War, General and Special Staff, RG 165

Chapter 1

1. Interview with Issei Nishimori, Nagasaki, June 16, 1978.
2. Interview with Sueo Inoue, Nagasaki, June 16, 1978.
3. Interview with Tsukasa Uchida, Nagasaki, June 21, 1978.
4. Interview with Hideo Matsuno, Nagasaki, June 20, 1978.
5. Interview with Sadako Kurihara, Hiroshima, June 26, 1978.
6. *The Chrysanthemum and the Sword* (1946) by the anthropologist Ruth Benedict was regarded as an authoritative source on Japanese society. Andrew Roth's *Dilemma in Japan* (1945) was also widely read. In *American Attitudes toward Japan 1941–1975*, Sheila Johnson discusses the impressions of the American public about Japan.

Chapter 2

1. *Foreign Relations of the United States 1945* (hereafter *FRUS*), 6:621–24.
2. Folder 000.71, Releasing Information, decimal files 1942–1948, MED. This was in contrast to American public opinion. According to a Gallup poll at the end of 1944, 13 percent of the Americans questioned favored the extermination of Japan. In 1945, 54 percent of those questioned approved of the dropping of the atomic bombs; 23 percent said more atom bombs should have been dropped before Japan was given a chance to surrender. Stephen Harper, *Miracle of Deliverance*, p. 202.
3. Robert J. C. Butow, *Japan's Decision to Surrender*, p. 150.
4. Fletcher Knebel and Charles W. Bailey II, *No High Ground*, p. 147.
5. Ibid., p. 153.
6. Butow, *Japan's Decision to Surrender*, pp. 150–51.
7. Toshikazu Kase, *Journey to the Missouri*, p. 213. Regarding the number of dead and injured in the two atomic bombings, several estimates exist. The total population of the cities at the time of the bombings is not known, partly because the number of soldiers was secret, many schoolchildren had been evacuated, and Korean forced laborers were not strictly counted. To this day, it is not known how many Koreans were killed or injured, and no official attempt has been made to find out. According to the report of the cities of Hiroshima and Nagasaki to the United Nations in 1976, however, the number of dead in Hiroshima by the end of December 1945 was 140,000 (± 10,000) and in Nagasaki 70,000 (± 10,000). In 1965 the Japanese government for the first time conducted a survey of exposed survivors. The number came to 277,955.
8. Dan Kurzman, *Day of the Bomb: Countdown to Hiroshima*, p. 419.
9. Glenn Hook, *Roots of Nuclearism: Censorship and Reportage of Atomic Damage in Hiroshima and Nagasaki*, pp. 136–37.
10. Robert Trumbull, *Nine Who Survived Hiroshima and Nagasaki*, pp. 91–92.
11. Interview with Hideo Matsuno, Domei editor in Nagasaki in August 1945, June 20, 1978.
12. Hook, *Roots of Nuclearism*, p. 137.
13. *FRUS 1945*, 6:633.
14. Anthony Cave Brown and Charles B. MacDonald, eds., *The Secret History of the Atomic Bomb*, p. 532.
15. *FRUS 1945*, 6:633.
16. Censorship in Japan before the surrender in August 1945 was extremely rigid. Throughout the short history of public information in Japan, the press was restricted through different laws and practices. The so-called Meiji Restoration took place in 1868. It "Westernized" Japan, but at the same time it replaced the old order by a new one, which in many respects was no less strict. The press was immediately restricted to ensure support for the new government system. From 1868 onward, different security laws as well as laws establishing censorship and restricting free speech were imposed. New, amended, or extended laws on these subjects were introduced several times after that. In addition, the police had wide powers and could interpret the laws arbitrarily. Material intended for publication

was subject to precensorship or postcensorship, depending on the type of material. The rules changed from time to time, as did the interpretations. Punishments varied, but prison was common. In addition to laws directly concerned with the press, there was also the Peace Preservation Law, under which threat to public tranquility, an elastic description, could be cited.

During the 1930s, with the international situation becoming tenser and Japan's undertakings abroad ever more aggressive, the state did not limit itself to controlling the existing press through censorship. It also turned to supplying and, in the end, completely dominating information to be printed. In 1936 the Cabinet Information Committee was formed, and a completely state-run news agency, Domei, started providing news regarded as fit to print. The press now served as a propaganda medium for the government. This process was completed in December 1941, when it was declared that nothing could be published without an advance permit.

For some accounts of censorship in Japan before 1945, see Lawrence Ward Beer, *Freedom of Expression in Japan*; Saburo Ienaga, *The Pacific War 1931–1945*; Tomiko Kakegawa, *The Press and Public Opinion in Japan 1931–1941*; and Richard H. Mitchell, *Censorship in Imperial Japan*.

17. Translation of *Nagasaki shimbun* Accounts Pertaining to the Atomic Bombings of Hiroshima and Nagasaki, March 14, 1946, USSBS 3F Doc. (3)2.

18. Summary no. 1239, 16.8.45, SRS 1761, Magic.

19. Memo from Swiss Legation in charge of Japanese interests, urgent cable, communication from Japanese government, *FRUS 1945* 6:472–73. This memo caused the U. S. Special War Problems Division to send an inquiry to the chairman of the State-War-Navy Coordinating Committee asking for guidance on how to react to the Japanese accusation. The inquiry was made on September 5, three weeks after the Japanese message was received. It took until October 24, following some discussion, for the Department of State to send its answer. This consisted of one short sentence with no further comments acknowledging the receipt of the memo "concerning the alleged bombing on August 6, 1945, of the town of Hiroshima by United States airplane" *(FRUS 1945* 6:474).

20. Hook, *Roots of Nuclearism*, p. 138.

21. Ibid., pp. 138–39.

22. Quoted in John Toland, *The Rising Sun*, p. 945.

23. Hook, *Roots of Nuclearism*, p. 142.

24. Ibid., p. 143.

25. Ibid., p. 141.

26. Summary no. 1239, 16.8.45, SRS 1761, Magic.

27. Folder 000.71, Releasing Information, decimal files 1942–1948, MED.

28. William J. Coughlin, *Conquered Press*, p. 3.

29. Ibid., p. 4.

Chapter 3

1. There are many detailed accounts of American planning for the Occupation. Hugh Borton, himself a participant in State Department planning, is the author of *American Presurrender Planning for Postwar Japan*.

2. Jun Eto has traced the planning of censorship by Byron Price in *Occupation Censorship and Postwar Japan*.

3. Letter to Byron Price, Director, Office of Censorship, from Secretary of War Henry L. Stimson, September 29, 1943, JCS 873, May 24, 1944, appendix B, folder CCS 000.76 (6–26–43), sec. 1, JCS.

4. Ibid.

5. Letter to Price from Assistant Secretary of State Adolf A. Berle, October 5, 1943, ibid., appendix A.

6. Censorship of Civilian Communications in the Pacific-Asiatic Theaters, memorandum by Director of Civil Affairs Division, War Department, enclosure to JCS 873/1, June 10, 1944, folder CCS 000.76 (6–26–43), sec. 1, JCS.

7. Censorship of Civilian Communications in Areas Occupied or Controlled by Military Authorities. War Department to Commander in Chief, South-West Pacific Area, May 19, 1944, ibid., appendix B.

8. Censorship of Civilian Communications in Areas Occupied or Controlled by the Armed Forces, ibid., annex to appendix B.

9. Proposed letter to Director of Office of Censorship from the Joint Chiefs of Staff, ibid.

10. Letter from Director of Office of Censorship to Admiral William D. Leahy, Chief of Staff, September 11, 1944, JCS 873/2, September 25, 1944, ibid.

11. Draft letter to Director of Office of Censorship, ibid.

12. Appendix to sec. 2, JCS 873/3, November 12, 1944, ibid.

13. Annex to appendix to JCS 873/3, ibid.

14. Political Directive for Military Government in the Japanese Outlying Islands, January 12, 1945, JCS 1231, loose, box 8550, SCAP.

15. Army Forces in Far East Basic Plan for Civilian Censorship in Japan, April 20, 1945, box 8517, SCAP.

16. Responsibility for Civilian Censorship in Japan, decision on JCS 1353, May 24, 1945, CCS 000.73, Japan (5–16–45), JCS.

17. Revised AFPAC Basic Plan for Civil Censorship in Japan, box 55, AS.

18. Akira Iriye, *Continuities in U.S.-Japanese Relations 1941–1949*, pp. 380–81.

19. POLAD to Secretary of State, March 17, 1948, The political adviser to SCAP, W. J. Sebald, took the opportunity in this message concerning another question to vent his frustration with SCAP: "it would appear that this mission, in its capacity as Diplomatic Section of this Head Quarters, is precluded from exclusive exploitation of any intelligence material and record in Japan unless a request is made. . . . The Assistant Chief of Staff, G-2 . . . would prohibit all objective reporting on the part of this Mission. . . . it is not my intention to raise this question with the Supreme Commander in view of possible misunderstanding to which any conceivable approach on this subject might give rise. . . . by the integration of this Mission into GHQ its freedom of operation in the normal sense was largely lost." *FRUS 1948*, 6:684–85.

20. *FRUS 1944*, 5:1213–14.

21. Iriye, *Continuities in U.S.-Japanese Relations*, p. 390.

22. Ibid., p. 391.

23. *Political Reorientation of Japan*, 2:423–26.

24. Potsdam Declaration, cited in *Political Reorientation of Japan*. The Soviet Union, which had not yet declared war on Japan, did not take part in the declaration.

25. SCAPIN 16, September 10, 1945, box 8553, SCAP.

26. SCAPIN 51, September 24, 1945, box 8553, SCAP.

27. SCAPIN 66, September 27, 1945, box 8553, SCAP.

28. Memorandum from Civil Censorship Detachment to the Office of the Chief of Counter-Intelligence, Civil Censorship Detachment, September 29, 1945, folder 000.73, Press Censorship, July 1944–September 1946, box 8520, SCAP; Coughlin, *Conquered Press*, pp. 24–26.

29. Coughlin, *Conquered Press*, p. 65.

30. Jun Eto, in *Occupation Censorship and Postwar Japan*, has pointed out the driving force of the director of the Office of Censorship. Eto advances the thesis that censorship was, in the end, a civilian undertaking, and that President Franklin Roosevelt was ultimately responsible for its introduction. He sees U.S. censorship as part of a concerted plan to remold Japan by attacking the very roots of its culture—the language. Under this plan, according to Eto, civilian censorship was an important step toward making Japan more "transparent," meaning more easily understandable, and consequently more easily controlled and directed. Eto has written several articles on this subject, which are listed in the bibliography.

Chapter 4

1. Instructions to General of the Army Douglas MacArthur from the Joint Chiefs of Staff, SWNCC 181/2, folder 740.00119 Control (Japan) 9-1345, SD.

2. United States Presidential Basic Initial Post-Surrender Directive issued to the Supreme Commander for the Allied Powers, November 8, 1945, reprinted in *Political Reorientation of Japan*. On August 29 MacArthur had received a summary of this directive.

3. Herbert Feis, *Japan Subdued*, p. 23.

4. Merle Fainsod, *Military Government and the Occupation of Japan*, cited in *Japan's Prospects*, ed. D. G. Haring, pp. 288–91.

5. Charles Willoughby, ed., *SCAP*, vol. 1 supplement: *MacArthur in Japan*, pp. 71–73.

6. Charles Willoughby, *MacArthur 1941–1951: Victory in the Pacific*, p. 322.

7. Ibid.

8. For the organization of Supreme Commander of Allied Powers Headquarters and of the Civil Intelligence Section, see figure 1.

9. Press, Pictorial and Broadcast Section Precensorship of News, October 17, 1945, folder Press Censorship July 1944–September 1946, box 8520, SCAP.

10. General Plan for Civil Censorship in Japan, 1944, box 55, AS.

11. SCAPIN 16, September 10, 1945, box 8553, SCAP.

12. Civil Censorship Detachment Memorandum, September 11, 1945, PPB History, box 8569, SCAP.

13. Akihiko Haruhara, *The Impact of the Occupation on the Japanese Press*, p. 13.

14. Kokichi Takakuwa, *MacArthur no shimbun kenetsu.*

15. Joseph L. Marx, *Nagasaki, the Necessary Bomb?*, pp. 81–85. Also author's interview with Hideo Matsuno, Nagasaki, June 20, 1978.

16. Butow, *Japan's Decision to Surrender*, p. 186.

17. Telegram from Commander in Chief of the Army Forces in the Pacific, September 10, 1945, folder Outgoing Messages 1941–1946, Civil Censorship Detachment Administrative File, box 8549, SCAP.

18. *Manual of PPB: Censorship in Japan*, CCD, September 30, 1945, box 8569, SCAP.

19. Summary no. 1255, September 13, 1945, SRS 1777, Magic.

20. Telegram from Commander in Chief of Army Forces in the Pacific, September 10, 1945.

21. Civil Censorship officer statement to representatives of Japanese press and radio re: Censorship on Behalf of the Supreme Commander, Press, Pictorial and Broadcast Section Manual, September 30, 1945, box 8569, SCAP.

22. Coughlin, *Conquered Press*, p. 33.

23. Telegram from Commander in Chief of the Army Forces in the Pacific, September 10, 1945.

24. September 23, 1945, PPB History, box 8569, SCAP.

25. Ibid., October 31, 1945.

26. SCAPIN 34, September 18, 1945, box 8553, SCAP.

27. SCAPIN 33 (Press Code for Japan), September 18, 1945, box 8553, SCAP.

28. Civil Censorship Detachment instructions to publishers. Author's copy from Hiroshima publisher.

29. Memorandum for Office of Chief of Counter-Intelligence regarding press censorship policy in Japan, November 10, 1945, box 8654, SCAP.

30. Check sheet from Civil Censorship Detachment to Office of the Chief of Counter-Intelligence regarding Censorship of Information Media, November 7, 1945, PPB History, box 8569, SCAP.

31. SCAPIN 37 (Suspension of Tokyo newspaper *Nippon Times*), September 19, 1945, box 8553, SCAP. Reasons explained in folder 000.73 Press Censorship July 1944–September 1946, box 8520, SCAP.

32. PPB History, box 8569, SCAP.

33. Ibid., check sheet from PPB District II to PPB Division, June 14, 1948.

34. SCAPIN 733, February 13, 1946, box 8553, SCAP.

35. September 23, 1945, PPB History, box 8569, SCAP.

36. Ibid.

37. SCAPIN 658, box 8553, SCAP. For results of campaign to collect titles of motion pictures existing, see note 31.

38. See note 31.

39. Memorandum of the Postal Division for Office of the Chief of Counter-Intelligence Regarding Activation of Postal Censorship, September 13, 1945, *The Supreme Commander for the Allied Powers: Reports of General MacArthur*, p. 238.

40. Mission of the Civil Censorship Detachment, file III, funds for FY 47, 48, 49, box 8523, SCAP.

41. CCD, box 8517, SCAP.

42. Fainsod, *Military Government and the Occupation of Japan*, p. 294. The Four Freedoms, among which was freedom of speech, were declared by President Franklin D. Roosevelt in a speech to the U.S. Congress in January 1941, where he described as the goal of the Allies "the democratization of the world."

43. Check sheet from the Office of the Chief of Counter-Intelligence to the Civil Information and Education Section, February 5, 1946, PPB History, box 8569, SCAP.

44. Mark Gayn, *Japan Diary*, p. 69.

Chapter 5

1. Akira Iriye, *Continuities in U.S.-Japanese Relations 1941–1949*, p. 388.

2. Roger Buckley, *Occupation Diplomacy*, p. 9.

3. Iriye, *Continuities in U.S.-Japanese Relations*, p. 392.

4. Ibid., p. 395.

5. Herbert Feis, *Japan Subdued*, p. 52.

6. Iriye, *Continuities in U.S.-Japanese Relations*, p. 391.

7. Ibid., p. 395.

8. Harry Truman, *Year of Decision*, pp. 431–32.

9. Feis, *Japan Subdued*, pp. 122–25.

10. Ibid., pp. 148–49.

11. L. H. Foulds, Far Eastern expert in the Foreign Office, quoted in Iriye, *Continuities in U.S.-Japanese Relations*, p. 397.

12. *FRUS* 1945, 6:535.

13. Herbert Feis, *Contest over Japan*, appendix.

14. *FRUS 1947*, 6:234.

15. *FRUS 1946*, 8:307–9.

16. *FRUS 1947*, 6:214–16.

17. Willoughby, *MacArthur 1941–1951*, p. 317.

18. W. MacMahon Ball, *Japan: Enemy or Ally?*, p. 23.

19. Ibid., p. 33.

20. Gayn, *Japan Diary*, p. 301.

21. State Department regarding United States Policy toward Japan, May 21, 1948, folder 740.00119/4-2848 Control (Japan), SD.

22. *FRUS 1945*, 6:790–91.

23. Ibid., 6:794.

24. *FRUS 1946*, 8:285.

25. POLAD to State Department and United States Embassy in Moscow regarding Allied Council/Derevyanko, folder 740.00119/9-1346 Control (Japan), SD.

26. Minutes of Allied Council meeting, October 1947, box 21, SCAP.

27. Minutes of Allied Council meeting, July 27, 1946, box 20, SCAP.

28. POLAD to Secretary of State regarding Confiscation of All Fascist, Militaristic, and Anti-Allied Literature in Japan, August 5, 1946, folder 740.00119/8-546 Control (Japan), SD.

29. See chapter 8.

30. Jun Eto, *Occupation Censorship and Postwar Japan.*

Chapter 6

1. Original document owned by Sadako Kurihara.

2. Operational Jurisdiction and Place Map of Japan and Korea prior to May 3, 1946, Civil Censorship Detachment, box 8523, SCAP.

3. Standing Operation Procedure and Distribution of Work, May 1, 1947, CCD District II, Press, Pictorial and Broadcasting Section [*sic*], New Agency sub-section, box 8523, SCAP.

4. Ibid.

5. Ibid.

6. Jun Eto, *The Occupation Censorship and Postwar Japan.*

7. Ibid.

8. Position Description, War Department Field Service, undated, box 8523, SCAP.

9. Ibid.

10. Mission of CCD, box 8523, SCAP.

11. Pre-Censorship and Post-Censorship, PPB Central File, no date, box 8576, SCAP.

12. CCD to CIS: Changes Effected in PPB units in Tokyo, October 12, 1946, PPB History, box 8569, SCAP.

13. CCD Work Load Factors, CCD Administrative Division File no. 111, box 8523, SCAP.

14. PPB History, March 30, 1948, box 8569, SCAP, and Temporary Key Log, CCD, December 6, 1947, file 000.76, Key Logs and Supplements, box 8654, SCAP.

15. *Manual of PPB: Censorship in Japan*, September 30, 1945, CCD, Army Forces in the Pacific, box 8569, SCAP.

16. Office of the Chief of Counter-Intelligence, September 3, 1945, box 8520, SCAP.

17. Ibid.

18. PPB file, Censorship of Foreign Publications, box 8654, SCAP.

19. PPB Monthly Operations Report, annex 1, November 25, 1946, file 211, box 8568, SCAP.

20. Dissemination of Civil Censorship Intercepts, The Adjutant General's Office to GHQ, USAFPAC, Office of the Chief of Counter-Intelligence, January 31, 1946, box 8524, SCAP.

21. Subject Matter Guide for Use by Civil Censorship under United States Jurisdiction Overseas, January 1946, GHQ, USAFPAC, OCCI, CCD, box 8524, SCAP.

22. Ibid. After the declassification of SCAP records, several researchers discovered material showing the keen American interest in this subject.

23. Examiner's Requirements Guide, September 26, 1945. GHQ, USAFPAC, OCCI, CCD, box 8524, SCAP.

24. Subject Matter Guide for PPB, September 10, 1945, GHQ, OCCI, CCD, file 300.6 Secret CIS, box 8654, SCAP.

25. The interception of private mail led to many tragedies. One intercept, which I found in the SCAP Records, consisted of two letters. One was written on thin, light green rice paper, folded in the Japanese way, tied with a ribbon, and unopened. The other letter was written in English. It was from a woman and she addressed the letter to the Occupation authorities, asking them please to forward the accompanying letter to her husband, whom she had not seen since the beginning of the war and not heard from for several years. At the time of surrender he was commander on an island in the Pacific, and she was sure that he would be executed for war crimes. She wanted him to know that she was thinking of him and asked that this, her last message to him before his death, would be sent to him. The censors had not even checked the thin green letter, much less forwarded it.

Another letter was from a desolate girl in the rural Tohoku district. Her letter was to a man she earlier had been introduced to as a marriage prospect. She wrote that immediately upon meeting him she knew that she wanted to marry him and nobody else. After their meeting she at once wrote to tell him that she accepted his marriage proposal, but she did not receive a response. Later she heard that he was already married to somebody else. She was now writing to say that, because the censors had held up her letter to him, he had evidently thought that she was not interested and gone ahead to accept another arrangement. Convinced that he was the only man she wanted, she was left with no choice but to live out her life in loneliness.

A third intercept was from a nisei who had come to Japan just before the war and was caught there. There had been no way for him to communicate with his girlfriend in the United States. He now rushed to write to her that he still wanted to marry her, and he hoped that she had waited for him, too. The letter never passed the censors, because in the same letter the writer mentioned that he might stay a while longer in Japan to earn some money. He had been offered a job as a translator for Americans going to Hiroshima. The censor had noted "possibly unreliable" and left the letter in the files.

26. Key Log Supplement, January 2, 1948, file 000.76, key logs and supplement, CCD, box 8654, SCAP.

27. Ibid.

28. Jun Eto has given one account in *The Problem of Dependence*. Other Japanese researchers claim that the constitution was the result of bargaining between Prime Minister Shidehara and MacArthur, and that Shidehara convinced MacArthur to retain the emperor in return for the so-called war-renouncing Article 9. One of these researchers is Ikuhito Hata.

29. Key Log Addition, April 24, 1946, file 300.6 Secret, box 8654, SCAP.

30. Interview with Mr. Matsui, PPB, November 7, 1946, PPB History, box 8569, SCAP.

31. Suppressed Books PPB District I Report, May 24, 1946, file 200.11 Books Censorship 1946, box 8655, SCAP.

32. Five Sentences no ni yoru by Kunizo Yoshizaki [*sic*]. PPB Book Department. District III Delete Log September 29, 1947, Gordon W. Prange Collection.

33. Ibid.

34. Delete and Suppress Log, file 000.73, PPB Subsection Book Department, December 26, 1946, box 8655, SCAP.

35. Ultranationalism: Poems Advocating Nationalism. Collections of Poems by the Association Fuji Poem Circle, August 31, 1949, PPB, CCD, box 8570, SCAP.

36. Censorship of Book by United Press Correspondent, September 23, 1946, PPB to CCD, folder 000.73, Censorship of Foreign Publication, box 8654, SCAP.

37. Ibid.

38. *Hiroshima shimbun*, "They Slew or Sold Their Beloved Children," August 1, 1946, Chief PPB Fukuoka District, Gordon W. Prange Collection.

39. Ibid.

40. Nagai, *Horobinu mono o* (For an immortal thing), October 1, 1948, Gordon W. Prange Collection.

41. *Tori no apato,* Memorandum PPB District I, March 11, 1947, file 200.1, Books Censorship, CIS, box 8655, SCAP.

42. Coughlin, *Conquered Press*, p. 16.

43. Ibid., pp. 46–47.

44. Jun Eto, *One Aspect of the Allied Occupation of Japan: The Censorship Operation and Post-War Japanese Literature*. Eto describes in detail the censorship actions against the poem about the *Yamato*.

45. Protest by CCD censors against censorship regarding Key Log no. 1 on the Japanese constitution, June 19, 1946, file 000.73, Press Censorship July 1944–September 1946, CIS, box 8520, SCAP.

46. Instructions from CCD to Press and Radio Censors, September 10, 1945, *CCD Censorship History*, box 16, SCAP.

47. Check Sheet CCD to General Thorpe, file 311.7, January 19, 1946. Quoted in *CCD Censorship History*, box 16, SCAP.

48. Guidance on Small Publications, Chief PPB to PPB Fukuoka, May 16, 1946, file 300.6 Secret, CIS, box 8654, SCAP.

49. *CCD Censorship History*, box 16, SCAP.

50. *Hiroshima shimbun*, "An Escape from Death in Vladivostok," August 14, 1946. Memorandum from District Censor, PPB, Fukuoka. Gordon W. Prange Collection.

51. Definition of Flagrant Violations to Press Publications Censor from District Censor, PPB District One, Admin. Division Subject Files, Uyehara. September 20, 1948, box 17, SCAP.

In 1949 and 1950 the Occupation authorities attacked Japanese Communists and leftists. In the so-called Red Purge, persons with leftist leanings lost their jobs, whether in government or private industry. Among them were members of the Japan Communist Party and journalists on the staff of the party newspaper *Akahata*. General MacArthur also suggested that the Communist Party be outlawed. For more about the Red Purge, see Allan Cole, George Totten, and

Cecil Uyehara, *Socialist Parties in Postwar Japan.*

52. Coughlin, *Conquered Press*, p. 51.

53. From Col. Grove, CCD to G-2, May 20, 1949, CIS, box 8523, SCAP.

54. Revision of Press Code. CCD to CIS, April 14, 1947, PPB History, box 8569, SCAP.

55. Memorandum for the Chief of Staff from C. A. Willoughby, G-2, October 29, 1946, box 8538, SCAP.

56. Ibid.

57. Censorship of Sport Broadcasts. PPB Division to District Stations, April 20, 1946, PPB History, box 8569, SCAP.

58. Transfer of Newspapers and Agencies from Pre-Censorship to Post-Censorship, November 10, 1946, PPB Division File Abolition of Censorship, PPB District, box 8576, SCAP.

59. PPB Division, November 20, 1946, PPB History, box 8569, SCAP.

60. Political Registration No. 5-408, June 26, 1947, PPB History, box 8569, SCAP.

61. Political Registration No. 5-407. Ibid.

62. Memorandum for the Chief of Staff from C. A. Willoughby, G-2, October 29, 1946, box 8538, SCAP.

63. Chief of Staff to G-2, June 6, 1947, Appendix L: Modification of Censorship Controls in the Occupied Area, SCAP: *Reports of General MacArthur. MacArthur in Japan. The Occupation: Military Phase,* vol. V, supplement p. 239.

64. Ibid.

65. Post-Censorship of Broadcasts, G-2 to Chief of Staff, Memorandum, September 10, 1947, ibid.

66. Memorandum PPB Division, October 1, 1947, PPB History, box 8569, SCAP.

67. Gradually media were transferred to postcensorship. See note 63.

68. Telegram to General MacArthur: Pre-Censorship to Cease Immediately. Approved by President, October 9, 1948, file 740.0119 Control (Japan), box 3824, SD.

69. Coughlin, *Conquered Press*, p. 56.

70. Sey Nishimura, *Medical Censorship in Occupied Japan 1945–1948*, p. 13.

71. SCAP, *Reports of General MacArthur*, pp. 240–41.

72. Civil Censorship Decontrol, Chief of Staff to G-2, October 11, 1949, box 8539, SCAP.

73. SCAP, *Reports of General MacArthur*, p. 241.

74. For one account, see T. A. Bisson, *Prospects for Democracy in Japan.*

75. For one account, see Hans Baerwald, *The Purge of Japanese Leaders under the Occupation.*

76. *CCD Censorship History*, box 16, SCAP.

77. Ibid.

78. Ibid.

79. Ibid.

80. Ibid.

Chapter 7

1. Civil Censorship Plan approved by Chief of Staff, GHQ, April 20, 1945, box 8517, SCAP.

2. JCS 873/3, November 12, 1944, folder CCS 000.76 (6-26-43), sec. 1, JCS.

3. Office of the Chief of Counter-Intelligence to the Assistant Chief of Staff, G-2, War Department, September 30, 1945, file 319.1, box 55, AS.

4. Ibid.

5. Memorandum for the Japanese Government from SCAP, October 26, 1945, box 2275, SD/FS.

6. Memorandum from POLAD to Secretary of State, October 10, 1945, vol. VII, box 2275, SD/FS.

7. Civil Information and Education Section Press Analysis, November 9, 1945.

8. Press, Pictorial and Broadcasting [*sic*] District II to PPB Division, GHQ, October 30, 1945, folder 000.73 Press Censorship July 1944–September 1946, box 8520, SCAP.

9. PPB, CCD Memorandum for Record: Warning of Press Code Democratic News, August 10, 1949, box 8570, SCAP.

10. PPB Manual, September 30, 1945, quoting SCAP statement to the Japanese press and radio representatives, September 15, 1945, box 8569, SCAP.

11. PPB Memorandum, July 15, 1948, box 8576, SCAP.

12. In the *PPB History*, March 26, 1948, an example is cited regarding a book called *Defendant Tojo's Affidavit*. The foreword was judged "highly objectionable," and a "complete investigation" was undertaken. This resulted in the publisher being returned to precensorship and requested to withdraw all copies of the book. Renewed distribution could take place only after the offensive part was deleted from all copies. Box 8569, SCAP.

13. SCAP, *Reports of General MacArthur*, p. 240.

14. Ibid.

15. Draft of Directive to G-2 from Chief of Staff for Civil Censorship in Japan and Korea regarding Modification of Civil Censorship Controls in Occupied Areas, June 6, 1947, box 8524, SCAP.

16. *PPB History*, July 1, 1946, box 8569, SCAP.

17. Ibid., July 7, 1946.

18. Ibid., August 18, 1946.

19. CIE to G-2, April 5, 1948, folder 000.73 Violations of Press Code for 28.8.48–2.4.49, box 8520, SCAP.

20. G-2 to Chief of Staff, April 15, 1948, ibid.

21. CCD to Civil Intelligence Section, July 19, 1948, ibid.

22. Minutes of Joint Conference regarding Press Code Violations, February 3, 1949, ibid.

23. CIS to G-2, February 5, 1949, ibid.

24. Directive from the Chief of Staff regarding Prosecution of Flagrant Violations of Press Code for Japan, January 24, 1949, Administrative Division File, box 17, SCAP.

25. Press Code Violation Committed by *Red Flag (Akahata)*. CCD to G-2 April 2, 1949, folder 000.73 Violations of Press Code, August 28, 1948–April 2, 1949, box 8520, SCAP.

26. CCD to G-2, Joint Action on Flagrant Press Code Violation cases, April 29, 1949, ibid.

27. *CCD Censorship History*, box 16, SCAP.

28. Ibid.

29. Ibid.

30. Ibid.

Chapter 8

1. Manual of Press, Pictorial and Radio Broadcast Censorship in Japan September 30, 1945, Civil Censorship Detachment, Army Forces in the Pacific, box 8569, SCAP.

2. SCAPIN 34, September 18, 1945; SCAPIN 33, September 18, 1945, box 8553, SCAP.

3. SCAPIN 16, September 10, 1945, box 8553, SCAP.

4. History of Non-Military Activities of the Occupation of Japan 1945–19–, vol. XI, Social, Part B, Freedom of the Press (First Occupation Year), p. 18, box 8, SCAP.

5. Office of the Commander of Counter-Intelligence, GHQ, USAF PAC September 9, 1945, folder 319.1, box 55, AS. Also Akihiko Haruhara, *The Impact of the Occupation on the Japanese Press*, p. 12; Hook, *Roots of Nuclearism*, p. 141.

6. Coughlin, *Conquered Press*, pp. 21–22.

7. Wilfred Burchett, *Shadows of Hiroshima*. This is his own account of his reporting from Hiroshima and the consequences.

8. Ben Kiernan, ed., *Burchett Reporting the Other Side of the World 1939–1983*, p. 24.

9. Nagasaki Military Government Team to CCD, Fukuoka, March 18, 1947, Gordon W. Prange Collection.

10. Office of the District Censor, District Station III, CCD to Nagasaki Military Government Team, March 24, 1947, ibid.

11. Nagasaki Military Government Team to Commanding Officer, Kyushu Military Government Region, Fukuoka, June 27, 1947, ibid.

12. Office of the District Censor, District Station III, CCD to Commanding Officer, Kyushu Military Government Region, Fukuoka, July 17, 1947, ibid. On April 26, 1949, *Masako Does Not Collapse* was finally approved for publication. Daily Operational Report of the Publications Section, PPB, box 8684, SCAP.

13. Nagasaki is the only Japanese city that can be said to be influenced by Catholicism. It has also had relations with the Western world for several hundreds of years, even during the period when the rest of Japan was closed. That Nagasaki of all Japanese cities would be destroyed by an American atomic bomb was regarded as of special significance by many Christians there. Even the reactions to

the bombings differed. The expression "protesting Hiroshima, praying Nagasaki" was sometimes used, meaning that the survivors in Nagasaki sought a divine explanation for the atomic bombing.

14. The book was first called *The Bells Toll for Nagasaki* in English, but, when published, the name was changed to *The Bells of Nagasaki*. The quotation is from p. 107.

15. CCD to Civil Intelligence Section, May 15, 1947, folder 200.11 Book Censorship 1947, box 8655, SCAP.

16. Memorandum for Record PPB, CCD, January 12, 1947, regarding author of *Bells Toll for Nagasaki*, ibid.

17. Note from JJC to BJW (initials), ibid.

18. PPB to Civil Censorship Officer, December 26, 1947, ibid.

19. Memorandum for Record PPB, CCD, January 12, 1947, ibid.

20. PPB to Civil Censorship Officer, ibid.; PPB District I to PPB Division, undated, ibid. Dr. Takashi Nagai and Dr. Ryuzaburo Shikiba were put on watch-list on January 23, 1948. PPB file, box 8655, SCAP.

21. Colonel Bratton to General Willoughby re Censorship of Book on Bombing of Nagasaki, January 6, 1947, folder 200.11, Book Censorship 1947, box 8655, SCAP.

22. General Willoughby to Staff re Censorship of Book on Bombing of Nagasaki, January 10, 1948, folder 000.73 Censorship News Articles in Japanese Press, box 8519, SCAP.

23. Theater Intelligence to Colonel Bratton, January 12, 1948, ibid.

24. Colonel Bratton to General Willoughby, January 13, 1948, ibid.

25. CCD slip, January 13, 1948, ibid.

26. Memorandum for Record re Author of *The Bells Toll for Nagasaki*, January 16, 1948, folder 200.11 Book Censorship 1947, box 8655, SCAP.

27. Unnamed, undated document, ibid.

28. PPB Memorandum regarding publication of *The Bells Toll for Nagasaki*, February 10, 1948, ibid.

29. General Willoughby to Staff re Censorship of Book on Bombing of Nagasaki, March 21, 1948, ibid. "The Sack of Manila" was an account of atrocities committed by Japanese in the Philippine capital during the war.

30. CIS to G-2, undated, ibid.

31. Translation of letter from Dr. Shikiba, the publisher, undated, attached to (32), ibid.

32. CIS to G-2, March 29, 1948, ibid.

33. General Willoughby to Staff re Censorship of Book on Bombing of Nagasaki, March 31, 1948, folder 000.73 Censorship of News Articles in Japanese Press 1948, box 8519, SCAP.

34. Daily Diary of the Publications Section, February 9, 1949, PPB, box 8648, SCAP. On July 5, 1949, another book by Dr. Nagai, *Hanasaku oka* (Flowers on a hill), dealing with the reconstruction of Nagasaki "turning the bombed city into a hill of flowers," was approved in its entirety. On August 2 a third book by Nagai, *Experiencing the Atomic Bomb*, a description by the surviving pupils in a Nagasaki school of their experience of the bombing, was reported "for information," in the

Daily Activities Report of the Publications Section, July 5, 1949, and August 2, 1949. Box 8648, SCAP. List of Best-Selling Books, July 15, 1949, PPB, CCD folder APO 500, box 8570, SCAP.

35. *Manga bukku* by S. Kita and T. Nishi, January 22, 1947, folder 000.73 Delete and Suppress Books, box 8655, SCAP.

36. Undated, ibid.

37. Ibid.

38. *Yomiuri*, June 18, 1948, Gordon W. Prange Collection.

39. CCD to Deputy Chief, CIS, July 10, 1948, folder 000.73 Censorship News Articles in Japanese Press 1948, box 8519, SCAP.

40. PPB, CCD Memorandum re Censorship of Newspapers in Hiroshima July 27, 1948. Folder 000.71 Memo for Record (Costello). Box 8657. SCAP.

41. Press Analysis August 6 and August 30, 1948, Analysis and Research Division, CIE, GHQ, SCAP.

42. Information Slip, Press Code August 8, 1949, PPB, box 8570, SCAP.

43. Wayne P. Lammers and Osamu Masaoka, *Japanese A-Bomb Literature: An Annotated Bibliography*, and Monica Braw: *Den Censurerade Atombomben*.

44. Memorandum for Record re War Stories in Magazines, July 15, 1949, PPB, box 8570, SCAP.

45. CCD to CIS, March 27, 1947, folder 000.73, Censorship US Material, box 8520, SCAP.

46. *Asahi shimbun* News Item, CCD Report, September 18, 1946, folder Atomic Bomb Effects, box 7431, SCAP.

47. Kyodo News Precensored, November 8, 1947, ibid.

48. Kenzo Nakajima, ed., *Living Hiroshima*, p. 1.

49. CIS to G-2, folder 000.73 Censorship US Material 4.1.47–7.7.47, box 8520, SCAP.

50. CIS to Assistant Chief of Staff, G-2, re Censorship of United Press Article Submitted by *Mainichi Shimbun* December 28, 1946, folder 000.73 Censorship US Material 1945–46, CCD Admin., box 8520, SCAP.

51. *Nippon Times* agreement with the *New Yorker* attached to (52).

52. CCD to CCO, November 26, 1946, folder 300.6 Secret, box 8654, SCAP.

53. Associated Press News Item, undated, folder 200.1, Book Censorship 1947, box 8655, SCAP.

54. General MacArthur telegram to Oscar Hammerstein II, President of The Authors' League of America, re Censorship of Hersey and Snow, April 6, 1948, folder 000.73 Censorship of Foreign Publications, box 8654, SCAP.

55. Subject Matter Guide for Use by Civil Censors under United States Military Jurisdiction Overseas, Washington, D.C., January 31, 1946, box 8537, SCAP.

56. Edward Teller with Allen Brown, *The Legacy of Hiroshima* p. 223.

57. Smyth Report, in Anthony Cave Brown and Charles B. MacDonald, *The Secret History of the Atomic Bomb*, pp. 30–31.

58. Brown and MacDonald, *Secret History*, pp. 203–4.

59. James F. Byrnes, *Speaking Frankly*, pp. 261–62.

60. G. Richard Hewlett and Oscar E. Anderson, *A History of the United States*

Atomic Energy Commission, vol. 1: *The New World 1939/1946*, p. 354.

61. Burchett, *Shadows of Hiroshima*, pp. 19–20.

62. Hewlett and Anderson, *A History of the United States Atomic Energy Commission*, 1:580–81.

63. Groves to Stimson, July 18, 1945, quoted in Martin J. Sherwin, *A World Destroyed*, p. 223.

64. Merriman Smith, *Thank You Mr. President: A White House Notebook*, pp. 254–56.

65. Potsdam Papers, Document 1315, quoted in Herbert Feis, *Japan Subdued*, pp. 111–12.

66. Report on Overseas Operation—Atomic Bomb, Farrell to Groves, September 27, 1945, in Brown and MacDonald, *Secret History*, pp. 531–32.

67. Bush and Conant to Secretary of War, September 30, 1944, OSRD, folder no. 10, International Control of Atomic Energy, TS Manhattan Project File 1942–1946, MED.

68. Brown and MacDonald, *Secret History*, pp. xviii–xix.

69. Feis, *Japan Subdued*, pp. 117–18.

70. Gar Alperowitz, *Atomic Diplomacy*, p. 195.

71. Note to Editor, Confidential, Not for Publication, September 14, 1945, Press Branch, Bureau of Public Relations, War Department, folder 5B, TS Manhattan Project File 1942–1946, MED.

72. Folder 380.01, Publications, decimal files 1942–1948, MED.

73. Harry S. Truman Memorandum to War Department, August 30, 1945, folder 5B, TS Manhattan Project File 1942–1946, MED.

74. Louis Liebovich, *The Press and the Origins of the Cold War 1944–1947*, pp. 87–90.

75. Joint Chiefs of Staff JCS series Release of Information Regarding Atomic Bomb, August 17, 1945, folder ABC 471.6 Atom (17 Aug 45), sec. 1, WD.

76. Atomic Energy Act, AEC folder, box 7433, SCAP.

77. President Truman to Baruch, United States representative at the United Nations, August 15, 1946, folder 008, decimal files 1942–48. MED.

78. General Groves to Chief of Staff re Security of Information Concerning the Atomic Bomb, February 21, 1946, folder no. 12 Intelligence and Security, Manhattan Project File 1942–1946, MED.

79. United Press and Associated Press quoting Domei, Radio Tokyo, August 22, 1945, folder 000.71 Releasing Information, MED.

80. JCS 1501/2, February 22, 1946, Combined Chiefs of Staff 919/5, June 8, 1946, CCS 919/6, June 19, 1946, and JCS 919/7, June 22, 1946, folder 471.6 Atom (8-17-45), Sec 3-A, WD.

81. General Groves to AEC, December 9, 1946, folder 380.01 Declassification, decimal files 1942–48, MED.

82. Release of United States Department of Commerce, Office of Technical Services, January 22, 1947, folder AEC, box 7433, SCAP.

83. Memorandum Publicity re Army Participation in Atomic Energy Activities, folder 000.71 Releasing Information, decimal files 1942–48, MED.

84. "Subject Matter Guide for Use by Civil Censorships under United States Military Jurisdiction Overseas," Washington, D.C., January 31, 1946, box 8537, SCAP.

85. Temporary Key Log, December 6, 1947, folder 000.76 Key Logs and Supplements, box 8654, SCAP.

86. Temporary Key Log, December 31, 1947, ibid.

87. Key Log Supplement, Key Log Number 21, January 2, 1948, folder Key Log, ibid.

88. SCAP to Adj. General, Department of the Army, Information on Activities Having a Bearing on Nuclear Science and Atomic Energy, October 15, 1947, Atomic Energy Commission folder, box 7433, SCAP.

89. Memorandum Special Projects Unit, November 9, 1948, folder Publications, box 7431, SCAP.

90. Folder 000.73, Censorship News Articles in Japanese Press 1948, box 8519, SCAP.

91. Economic and Scientific Section to G-2, October 23, 1947, folder AEC, box 7433, SCAP.

92. Japanese reports can be found in boxes 7407 and 7408, SCAP, and in General Report of Atomic Bomb Casualty Commission, January 1947, National Research Council, JCS. They are also in Reports Pertaining to the Effects of the Atomic Bomb 1945–1946, MED.

93. William Johnston, introduction to Takashi Nagai, *The Bells of Nagasaki*.

94. Nagai, *The Bells of Nagasaki*, pp. 73–74.

95. Nishimura, *Medical Censorship*, p. 2.

96. Gayn, *Japan Diary*, p. 268.

97. Nishimura, *Medical Censorship*, pp. 7ff.

98. Ibid., p. 12.

99. Hiroshima and Nagasaki, p. 564.

100. SCAPIN 47, September 22, 1945, box 8553, SCAP.

101. WARX 79907, JCS to SCAP, October 30, 1945, CCS, folder 383.21 Japan (3-13-45) Sec 5, JCS.

102. WARX 88780, February 8, 1946, *FRUS 1946*, 8:147.

103. Policy for Research on Atomic Energy, Far Eastern Commission Records, FEC 024/1-6, August 9, 1946–January 14, 1947. CCD Administrative Division Incoming Messages January 1947–May 1949, box 8549, SCAP.

104. State-War-Navy Coordinating Committee Subcommittee Report re Publicity on Policy Regarding Japanese Atomic Energy Research, October 23, 1946, CCS, folder 383.21 Japan (3-13-45), sec. 14, JCS; Robert K. Wilcox, *Japan's Secret War: Japan's Race against Time to Build Its Own Atomic Bomb*, p. 192.

105. SCAP Memorandum to Japanese Government, May 27, 1949, rescinding Directive No. 3 SCAPIN 47, box 7410, SCAP.

106. Sasamoto, *Genbaku higaishodo chosa ni okeru*, p. 114ff.

107. Ibid., pp. 122–24.

108. General Report by ABCC, January 1947, to the National Research Council, JCS; Report on Medical Studies of the Effects of the Atomic Bomb by Dr. Masao Tsuzuki, Tokyo Imperial University, February 28, 1946, box 7406, SCAP.

109. Author's interview with Dr. Issei Nishimori, Nagasaki, June 16, 1978.

110. CCD Report of intercepted letter re Research on Physical Effects of Atomic Bomb, folder Atomic Bomb Effects, box 7431, SCAP.

111. SCAPIN 984 May 25, 1946, box 8553, SCAP. Comment in SCAP Activity Report September 1947–February 1948, JCS 1380/39, CCS 383.21 Japan (3-13-49) Sec 18, JCS.

112. Monthly Report June 1, 1946, in General Report of ABCC, January 1947, JCS; CCS folder 383.21, Japan (3-13-45) Sec 19, JCS. Masao Tsuzuki was professor of surgery at Tokyo Imperial University and an admiral in the Japanese Navy during the war. In the 1920s he studied the effects of radiation in the United States. He went to Hiroshima to study the effects of the atomic bomb at the end of August 1945 and became a liaison between Japanese scientists and American investigators. In 1947, however, he was purged from his position as professor because of his military record during the war.

113. Colonel Nichols to General Groves re Request for Project Data in Connection with Cancer Research, November 1, 1945, folder 000.71 Interchange of Information, decimal file 1942, MED.

114. Memorandum on Conference in Japan to Carry out Follow-up Studies on Atomic Bomb Casualties, November 4, 1946, box 7407, SCAP.

115. Memorandum on Long-time Follow-up on Atomic Bomb Casualties, November 14, 1946, box 7407, SCAP.

116. William S. Stone, Chairman, Army Medical Research and Development Board for the Surgeon General to General Groves, November–December 1946, box 8537, SCAP.

117. PPB Memorandum re Publication of Medical Articles on Atomic Bomb Research, January 2, 1947, folder 00.71, Memo for record Mr. Costello 1946–47, box 8656, SCAP.

118. SCAP Reports on Control and Surveillance of Atomic Energy Research and Development in Japan, November 1946–February 1947, JCS 1380/38, CCS 383.21 Japan (3-13-45) Sec 17, JCS.

119. ABCC 4th Report, July 7–July 13, 1947, box 7407, SCAP.

120. Melvin A. Block to Dr. Paul Henshaw, Representative in Japan of the Committee on Atomic Bomb Casualties, July 25 and September 22, 1947, box 7407, SCAP.

121. SCAP to JCS, Z17557, August 11, 1947, CCS 383.21 Japan (3-13-45) Sec 17, JCS.

122. AEC to Military Liaison Committee, November 3, 1947, CCS 383.21 Japan (3-13-45) Sec 18, JCS.

123. JCS 1380/42, November 8, 1947, ibid.

124. SCAP to JCS, January 27, 1948, ibid.

125. Memorandum of Conference on Declassification of Japanese Manuscripts and Opinion of Legal Section, SCAP, February 27 and March 11, 1948, folder AEC, box 7433, SCAP.

126. Memorandum for Secretary, Joint Civil Affairs Committee re Opinion Concerning Authority of SCAP from JCS, February 5, 1948, CCAC 014 Japan (9-20-44) Sec 5, JCS.

127. Joint Chiefs of Staff to MacArthur WAR 88233, August 26, 1948, CCS 383.21 Japan (3-13-45) Sec 19, JCS.

128. Memorandum of radiogram from SCAP Economic and Scientific Section to Department of Army, June 10, 1948, AEC folder, box 7433, SCAP.

129. Ibid. and radiogram from SCAP to JCS, June 21, 1948, ibid.

130. Joint Chiefs of Staff to MacArthur WAR 88233, August 26, 1948, CCS 383.21 Japan (3-13-45) Sec. 19, JCS. The emissary was a Lieutenant Colonel Cross.

131. Note for General Nichols, June 25, 1948, folder 371.2, Security and Intelligence, decimal files 1942–48, MED.

132. Memorandum from MLC to JCS, September 17, 1948, CCS 383.21 Japan (3-13-45) Sec 19, JCS.

133. JCS to SCAP, WAR 91882, November 1, 1948, JCS 1380/45, October 13, November 1948, CCS 389.21 Japan (3-13-45) Sec 20, JCS

134. Atomic Bombs Reports Declassified, box 8536, SCAP.

135. Activity Report, January 1949–April 1949, GHQ, SCAP. In JCS 1380/70, July 22, 1949, CCS 383.21 Japan (3-13-45) Sec 22, JCS.

136. Sasamoto, *Genbaku higaishodo chosa ni okeru.*

137. Hiroshima and Nagasaki, p. 554.

138. Sasamoto, *Genbaku higaishodo chosa ni okeru*, p. 137.

Chapter 9

1. Edward Teller with Allen Brown, *The Legacy of Hiroshima*, p. 213.

2. Report by Joint Strategic Survey Committee to Joint Chiefs of Staff, JCS 1477/1, October 30, 1945, Plans and Operations Division, ABC decimal file 1942–48, 471.6 Atom (8-17-45) Sec 2, AS.

3. Jun Eto has written, controversially, about this part of censorship. See his works cited in the bibliography.

4. War Guilt Campaign, Monthly Summation no. 1, October 5, 1945, SCAP: Summation of Non-Military Activities in Japan, p. 151.

5. Article by Kizo Kano, Purged Writer, Press, Pictorial and Broadcast Section III to PPB, folder Civil Censorship Detachment Administrative Division Purge Actions 000.73, box 8576, SCAP.

6. Office of the District Censor, District Station III, CCD to Commanding Officer, Kyushu Military Government Region HQ Fukuoka, July 16, 1947, Gordon W. Prange Collection.

7. Stimson diaries, July 21 and 24, 1945, quoted in Martin J. Sherwin, *A World Destroyed*, pp. 230–31.

8. William D. Leahy, *I Was There*, pp. 441–42.

9. Stimson diaries, May 1 and 16, 1945, quoted in Sherwin, *A World Destroyed*, pp. 195, 197.

10. Stimson, June 6, 1945, quoted in Fred Freed and Lew Giovannitti, *The Decision to Drop the Bomb*.

11. Memorandum from Undersecretary of the Navy Ralph Bard, in Sherwin, *A World Destroyed*, pp. 307–8.

12. Teller, *The Legacy of Hiroshima*, p. 22.

13. Franck Report, pp. 560–72, in Alice Kimball Smith, *A Peril and a Hope: The Scientists' Movement in America 1945–47*.

14. Albert Einstein plea, 1947, quoted in Max Morgan-Witts and Gordon Thomas, *Ruin from the Air*, p. 15. This letter never reached President Roosevelt. In a plea and a pamphlet, *Atomic War or Peace*, 1947, Einstein repeated his fear and presented a plan for world government. ABC decimal files 1942–1948, 471.6 Atom (8-17-45), box 570, sec. 7, Plans and Operations Division, AS.

15. Harry S. Truman, *Year of Decisions*, p. 302.

16. Memorandum for Secretary of War from George L. Harrison, May 1, 1945, in Sherwin, *A World Destroyed*, pp. 294–95.

17. Memorandum from Swiss Legation in Charge of Japanese Interests, communication from the Japanese Government, August 11, 1945, *FRUS 1945*, 6:472–73.

18. Radio Tokyo, August 10, 1945, in English-language transmission to Western North America.

19. Sasamoto, *Genbaku higaishodo chosa ni okeru*.

20. United Press quoting Radio Tokyo, August 24, 1945, folder 000.71 Releasing Information, MED.

21. Summary no. 1255, September 10, 1945, Diplomatic Summaries, SRS 1777, Magic.

22. Ibid., September 13, 1945.

23. Ibid., September 14 and 15, 1945.

24. Summary no. 1274, September 20, 1945, Diplomatic Summaries, SRS 1796, Magic.

Chapter 10

1. Gayn, *Japan Diary*, p. 122.

2. Sadao Asada, *Recent Works on the American Occupation of Japan: The State of the Art*, p. 179. Asada introduces different works on the subject of the relationship between Occupation and Japanese authorities.

3. T. J. Tempel, "The Tar Baby Target: 'Reform' of the Japanese Bureaucracy," in *Policy Planning during the Allied Occupation of Japan*, ed. Ward and Yoshikazu, p. 174.

4. Ball, *Japan: Enemy or Ally?*, p. 37.

5. Ibid., p. 17.

6. Coughlin, *Conquered Press*, p. 18.

7. Ibid., p. 117.

8. Ibid., p. 122.

9. Ibid., pp. 132–33.

10. Iriye, "Continuities in U.S.-Japanese Relations 1941–1949," in *The Origins of the Cold War in Asia*, ed. Iriye and Nagai.

11. Compton to Groves, Presentation to the American Public of Scientists' Views on Atomic Energy, August 23, 1948, and Statement to the Interim Committee on Post-War Security Policy, August 8, 1945, folder 334 Post-War Policy Committee, decimal file 1942–48, MED.

12. Teller, *The Legacy of Hiroshima*, pp. 31–32.

13. Published in Brown and MacDonald, eds., *Secret History*, pp. 127–28.

14. Seiji Imahori, *Gensuibaku jidai.*

BIBLIOGRAPHY

Primary Sources

A Decade of American Foreign Policy. Basic Documents. Washington, DC, 1950.

Baxter, James P. *Scientists against Time. Official History of the Office of Scientific Research Development 1940–1945*. Boston, 1952.

British Mission to Japan. *The Effects of the Atomic Bombings at Hiroshima and Nagasaki*. London, 1946.

Brown, Anthony Cave, and Charles B. MacDonald, eds. *The Secret History of the Atomic Bomb*. New York, 1977.

Foreign Relations of the United States 1944. Vol. 4. Washington, DC, 1969.

Foreign Relations of the United States 1945. Vol. 6. Washington, DC, 1969.

Foreign Relations of the United States 1946. Vol. 7. Washington, DC, 1971.

Foreign Relations of the United States 1947. Vol. 6. Washington, DC, 1972.

Foreign Relations of the United States 1948. Vol. 6. Washington, DC, 1974.

Foreign Relations of the United States 1949. Vol. 7, Part 2. Washington, DC, 1976.

Foreign Relations of the United States, The Conference at Berlin 1945. Vols. 1 and 2. Washington, DC, 1960.

Gordon W. Prange Collection. The East Asia Collection. McKelden Library. University of Maryland.

Hewlett, Richard G., and Oscar E. Anderson. *The New World 1939–1946: A History of the United States Atomic Energy Commission*. University Park, 1962.

Supreme Commander of the Allied Powers. *Analysis and Research Division Special Report*. N.p., 1949.

———. *A Brief Progress Report of the Political Reorganization of Japan*. N.p., 1949.

———. *Catalog of SCAP Directives*. Vols. 1 and 2. N.p., 1952.

———. *CI&E Bulletin: Press Analysis, Summaries*. N.d.

———. *The History of Intelligence Activities under General Douglas MacArthur 1942–1950*. N.p., n.d.

———. *Mission and Accomplishments of the Occupation in the Civil Information and Education Fields*. Tokyo, 1950.

———. *Mission and Accomplishments of the Occupation in the Economic and Scientific Fields*. Tokyo, 1952.

———. *Organization and Activities of General Headquarters* (also called *Selected Data on the Occupation of Japan*). Tokyo, 1950.

————. *Political Reorientation of Japan*. Washington, DC, 1950.

————. *Press Analysis by CI&E* (daily from October 23, 1945).

————. *Reports of General MacArthur in Japan: The Occupation*. Washington, DC, 1966.

————. *Selected Data on the Occupation of Japan and the Far East Command*. Tokyo, 1950.

————. *Summation of Non-Military Activities in Japan*. Monthly, 1945–1948.

————. *Two Years of Occupation*. Tokyo, 1948.

United States Atomic Energy Commission. *In the Matter of J. Robert Oppenheimer*. Transcript of Hearing before Personnel Security Board, April 12, 1954 through May 6, 1954. Washington, DC, 1954.

United States Department of State. *Activities of the Far Eastern Commission*. Report by the Secretary General February 26, 1947–July 10, 1947. Far Eastern Series no 24. Washington, DC, 1947.

————. *Occupation of Japan: Policy and Progress*. Publication 2671, Far East Series 17. Washington, DC, n.d.

————. *Our Occupation Policy for Japan*. Bulletin, October 7, 1945.

United States National Archives:

   Records of Allied Operational and Occupational Headquarters, World War II (Supreme Commander of the Allied Powers), Record Group 331.

   Records of the Department of the Army, RG 319.

   Records of the Department of State, General, RG 59.

   Records of the Department of State, Foreign Service Posts, RG 84.

   Records of the Department of State, State-War-Navy Coordinating Committee, RG 51.

   Records of the Department of War, RG 165.

   Records of the Far Eastern Commission 1945–1951, RG 43.

   Records of the House of Representatives, RG 233.

   Records of the Joint Chiefs of Staff, RG 218.

   Records of the Manhattan Engineering District, RG 77.

   Records of the National Security Agency, RG 457.

   Records of the Office of Censorship, RG 216.

   Records of the Office of Scientific Research and Development, Atomic Energy Commission, RG 227.

   Records of the Office of War Information, RG 208.

   Records of the United States Bombing Survey, RG 243.

United States Office of Censorship. *Code of Wartime Practices for the American Press*. Washington, DC, 1943.

United States Senate. Special Committee on Atomic Energy. *Hearings*. Washington, DC, 1946.

United States Strategic Bombing Survey. *The Effects of Atomic Bombs on Hiroshima and Nagasaki*. Washington, DC, 1946.

————. *Japan's Struggle to End the War*, edited by Walter Wilds. Washington, DC, 1946.

Whan, Vorin E., ed. *A Soldier Speaks: Public Papers and Speeches of*

General of the Army Douglas MacArthur. New York, 1965.

Interviews

Sueo Inoue, Nagasaki, June 16, 1978.
Sadako Kurihara, Hiroshima, June 26, 1978.
Hideo Matsuno, Nagasaki, June 20, 1978.
Issei Nishimori, Nagasaki, June 16, 1978.
Tsukasa Uchida, Nagasaki, June 21, 1978.

Secondary Sources

Acheson, Dean. *Present at the Creation: My Years at the State Department.* New York, 1969.
Aduard, Evert J. Lewe van. *Japan: From Surrender to Peace.* The Hague, 1953.
Alperowitz, Gar. *Atomic Diplomacy: Hiroshima and Potsdam.* New York, 1965.
Amakawa Akira and Eiji Takemae. *Nihon senryo hishi.* Vol. 1. Tokyo, 1977.
Arata Osada, comp.; Jean Dan and Ruth Sieben-Morgen, trans. *Children of the A-Bomb. Testament of the Boys and Girls of Hiroshima.* Tokyo, 1959.
Aruga Tadashi. "Sources in Japanese Archives and Libraries Relating to United States History." Tokyo, 1984.
Asada Sadao. "Recent Works on the American Occupation of Japan: The State of the Art." *The Japanese Journal of American Studies*, no. 1 (1981).
Baerwald, Hans H. *The Purge of Japan.* Berkeley and Los Angeles, 1959.
Baldwin, Hanson W. *Great Mistakes of the War. The Atomic Bomb: The Penalty for Expedience.* New York, 1950.
Ball, W. MacMahon. *Japan—Enemy or Ally?* New York, 1949.
Barrier, Gerald N. *Banned—Controversial Literature and Political Control in British India 1907–1947.* Columbia, 1974.
Barron, Jerome A. *Freedom of the Press for Whom?* Bloomington, 1973.
Beer, Lawrence Ward. *Freedom of Expression in Japan. A Study in Comparative Law, Politics and Society.* Tokyo, 1984.
Benedict, Ruth. *The Chrysanthemum and the Sword.* Boston, 1946.
Berkow, Robert H. "The Press in Postwar Japan." *Far Eastern Survey* 16, 14 (July 23, 1947).
Bisson, T. A. *Prospects for Democracy in Japan.* New York, 1949.
Blackett, P. M. S. *Fear, War and the Bomb.* New York, 1949.
Blair, Clay, Jr. *MacArthur.* London, 1977.
Borg, Dorothy, and Shumpei Okamoto, eds. *Pearl Harbor as History: Japanese-American Relations 1939–1941.* New York, 1972.
Borton, Hugh. *American Presurrender Planning for Postwar Japan.* New York, 1967.

Boyle, Michael J. "The Planning of the Occupation of Japan and the American Reform Tradition." Ph.D. dissertation, University of Wyoming, 1979.

Braw, Monica. "*Den Censurerade Atombomben*: En jämförelse av publicerad japansk atombombslitteratur under den amerikanska ockupationen av Japan 1945–1952 och perioden strax därefter 1952–1955." Paper presented at University of Lund, Sweden, 1979.

Brines, Russell. *MacArthur's Japan*. Philadelphia, 1948.

Brines, Russell, and W. J. Sebald. *With MacArthur in Japan*. New York, 1965.

Buckley, Roger. *Occupation Diplomacy: Britain, The United States and Japan 1945–1952*. Cambridge, England, 1982.

Burchett, Wilfred. *Shadows of Hiroshima*. London, 1983.

Butow, Robert J. C. *Japan's Decision to Surrender*. Stanford, 1954.

Byrnes, James F. *All in One Lifetime*. New York, 1958.

———. *Speaking Frankly*. New York, 1947.

Cary, Otis, ed. *From a Ruined Empire. Letters—Japan, China, Korea 1945–46*. Tokyo, 1975.

Clark, Hugh V. *Last Stop Nagasaki*. Sydney, 1984.

Cole, Allan B., George O. Totten, and Cecil H. Uyehara. *Socialist Parties in Postwar Japan*. New Haven, 1966.

Committee for the Compilation of Materials on Damage Caused by the Atomic Bombs in Hiroshima and Nagasaki. *Hiroshima and Nagasaki*. Tokyo 1981.

Compton, Arthur Holly. *Atomic Quest*. New York, 1956.

Coughlin, W. J. *Conquered Press: The MacArthur Era in Japanese Journalism*. Palo Alto, 1952.

Craig, William. *The Fall of Japan*. London, 1970.

Dallek, Robert. *Franklin D. Roosevelt and American Foreign Policy, 1932–1945*. New York, 1979.

Dewhirst, Martin, and Robert Farrell, eds. *The Soviet Censorship*. New Jersey, 1973.

Dower, John. "Occupied Japan and the American Lake, 1945–1950." In *America's Asia: Dissenting Essays on Asian-American Relations*, edited by Edward Friedman and Mark Selden. New York, 1971.

———. "Occupied Japan as History and Occupation History as Politics." *Journal of Asian Studies* 34 (1975).

———. *War Without Mercy. Race and Power in the Pacific War*. New York, 1986.

Eto Jun. "The Civil Censorship in Occupied Japan." *Hikaku bunka zasshi: The Annual of Comparative Culture*. Vol. 1. Tokyo Institute of Technology. Tokyo, 1982.

———. "The Constraints of the 1946 Constitution." *Japan Echo* 8, 1 (1981).

———. "Occupation Censorship and Postwar Japan." Part 1 (in English). *Hikaku bunka zasshi: The Annual of Comparative Culture*. Vol. 3. Tokyo Institute of Technology. Tokyo 1984. Part 2 (in Japanese). *Shokun* (December 1982; July, October, and November 1984).

———. *One Aspect of the Allied Occupation of Japan: The Censorship Oper-*

ation and Postwar Japanese Literature. Occasional Paper no. 8, East Asia Program, Wilson Center. Washington, DC, June 1980.

————. *The Problem of Dependence*. Occasional Paper no. 4, East Asia Program, Wilson Center. Washington, DC, March 1980.

————. "Reflections upon the Allied Occupation of Japan." Paper presented at the Foreign Service Institute, Washington, DC, 1979.

————. "The Severed Tie with the Past: Literature and the Occupation Period. The Case of Yoshida Mitsuru and the Last of the Battleship Yamato." Paper presented at the Wilson Center, Washington, DC, 1979.

Fainsod, Merle. "Military Government and the Occupation of Japan." In *Japan's Prospects*, edited by D. G. Haring. Cambridge, 1946.

Fearsey, Robert. *The Occupation of Japan. Second Phase 1948–1950*. London, 1950.

Feis, Herbert. *Japan Subdued* (also published as *The Atomic Bomb and the End of World War II*). Princeton, 1961.

————. *Contest over Japan*. New York, 1968.

Fischer, Heinz-Dietrich. *Pressekonzentration und Zensurpraxis im Ersten Weltkrieg*. Berlin, 1973.

Fisher, Phyllis K. *Los Alamos Experience*. Tokyo, 1985.

Fogelman, Edwin. *Hiroshima: The Decision to Use the A-Bomb*. New York, 1964.

Fontaine, Andre. *History of the Cold War*. New York, 1969.

Fredricks, Edgar J. *MacArthur: His Mission and Meaning*. Philadelphia, 1968.

Freed, Fred, and Lew Giovannitti. *The Decision to Drop the Bomb*. New York, 1965.

Fukushima Jyuro. "Senryo shoki ni okeru shimbun seisaku." In *Nippon senryogun, sono hikari to kage*. Tokyo, 1978.

————. "Senryoka ni okeru kenetsu. Seisaku to sono jittai." In *Senryoki Nippon no keizai to seiji*, edited by Takahide Nakamura. Tokyo, 1979.

Ganoe, William. *MacArthur Close-up: Much Then and Some Now*. New York, 1962.

Gayn, Mark. *Japan Diary*. Tokyo, 1981.

Genbaku Kankei Bunkan. Catalog of Bibliography of the Atomic Bomb. Hiroshima, 1960.

Glazer, Nathan. "From Ruth Benedict to Herman Kahn: The Postwar Japanese Image in the American Mind." In *The American Occupation of Japan: A Retrospective View*, edited by Grant Goodman. Lawrence, 1968.

Gluck, Carol, "Entangling Illusions—Japanese and American Views of the Occupation." In *New Frontiers in American–East Asian Relations*, edited by Warren Cohen. New York, 1983.

Goodman, Grant, ed. *The American Occupation of Japan: A Retrospective View*. Lawrence, 1968.

Gowing, Margret. *Britain and Atomic Energy*. London, 1964.

Grew, Joseph C. *Ten Years in Japan*. New York, 1944.

————. *Turbulent Era*. Boston, 1952.

Greyerz, Walo von. *Människan och kriget*. Stockholm, 1969.

Groves, Leslie. *Now It Can Be Told*. New York, 1962.

Gunther, John. *The Riddle of MacArthur: Japan, Korea and the Far East*. New York, 1951.

Hachiya Michihiko. *Hiroshima Diary. The Journal of a Japanese Physician August 6–September 30, 1945*. Chapel Hill, 1955.

Haring, D. G., ed. *Japan's Prospects*. Cambridge, 1946.

Harper, Stephen. *Miracle of Deliverance. The Case for the Bombing of Hiroshima and Nagasaki*. London, 1985.

Haruhara Akihiko. "The Impact of the Occupation on the Japanese Press." Paper presented at MacArthur Memorial Symposium, Norfolk, Virginia, October 18, 1984.

———. "Senryo kenetsu no ito to jittai 1–3." *Shimbun kenkyu*, nos. 6–8 (1984).

Hata Ikuhiko. *Amerika no tai-Nichi senryo seisaku*. Tokyo, 1976.

———. "Japan under the Occupation." *Japan Interpreter* 10 (1976).

———. "The Postwar Period in Retrospect." *Japan Echo* 11 (1984).

Hata Ikuhiko and Sodei Rinjiro. *Nihon senryo hishi*. Vol. 2. Tokyo, 1977.

Herken, Gregg. *The Winning Weapon. The Atomic Bomb in the Cold War 1945–1950*. New York, 1980.

Hersey, John. *Hiroshima*. New York, 1946

Hidaka Rokuro. *The Price of Affluence: Dilemmas of Contemporary Japan*. New York, 1985.

Hook, Glenn D. "Roots of Nuclearism: Censorship and Reportage of Atomic Damage in Hiroshima and Nagasaki." *Multilingua* 7, 1/2 (1988).

Hopewell, Jim. "Press Censorship: A Case Study." *Argus* 6, 6 (May 1971).

Huff, Sidney L., with Joe A. Morris. *My Fifteen Years with General MacArthur*. New York, 1964.

Huie, William B. *The Hiroshima Pilot*. New York, 1964.

Ienaga Saburo. *The Pacific War 1931–1945*. New York, 1978.

Imahori Seiji *Gensuibaku jidai*. Tokyo, 1960.

Imahori Seiji, Tsuruji Kotani, and Naomi Shohno. *Steps toward Peace*. Hiroshima, 1969.

Irie Takanori. "The Lingering Impact of Misguided Occupation Policies." *Japan Echo* 11 (1984).

Iriye, Akira. "Continuities in U.S.–Japanese Relations 1941–1949." In *The Origins of the Cold War in Asia*, edited by Akira Iriye and Yonosuke Nagai. Tokyo, 1977.

———. *Power and Culture: The Japanese-American War 1941–1945*. Cambridge, MA, 1981.

———, ed. *Mutual Images: Essays in American–Japanese Relations*. Cambridge, MA, 1975.

Ishizaka Kyu. "Tainichi genronseisaku to SWNC." NHK Report on Broadcast Research. Tokyo, June 1980.

Iwamatsu Shigetoshi. *Hankaku to senso sekinin: "Higaisha" Nihon to "kagaisha" Nihon*. Tokyo, 1982.

————. *Heiwa e no kohatsu: Bertrand Russell to Nagasaki.* Tokyo, 1982.

————. "A Perspective on the War Crimes." *The Bulletin of the Atomic Scientists* (February 1982).

Janis, Irving L. *Psychological Effects of the Atomic Attacks on Japan.* Santa Monica, 1950.

Johnson, Sheila K. *American Attitudes toward Japan 1941–1975.* Washington, DC, 1975.

Julian, Allen Phelps. *MacArthur: The Life of a General.* New York, 1963.

Jungk, Robert. *Strålar ur askan.* Stockholm, 1960.

Kakegawa Tomiko. "The Press and Public Opinion in Japan 1931–1941." In *Pearl Harbor as History.* Edited by Dorothy Borg and Shumpei Okamoto. New York, 1972.

Kase Toshikasu. *Journey to the Missouri: Invitation to Surrender.* New Haven, 1950.

Kato Masuo. *The Lost War.* New York, 1946.

Kawai Kazuo. *Japan's American Interlude.* Chicago, 1960.

Kelley, Frank R., and Cornelius Ryan. *MacArthur, Man of Action.* New York, 1950.

Kennan, George. *Memoirs 1925–1950.* Boston, 1967.

————. *The Nuclear Delusion: Soviet-American Relations in the Atomic Age.* London, 1983.

————. *The Realities of American Foreign Policy.* Princeton, 1954.

Kiernan, Ben, ed. *Burchett Reporting the Other Side of the World 1939–1983.* London, 1986.

Kilander, Svenbjörn. *Censur och Propaganda. Svensk informationspolitik under 1900-talets första decennier.* Stockholm, 1981.

Kissinger, Henry. *Nuclear Weapons and Foreign Policy.* New York, 1957.

Knebel, Fletcher, and Charles W. Bailey III. *No High Ground.* New York, 1960.

Kosaka Masataka. *100 Million Japanese: The Postwar Experience.* Tokyo, 1972.

Kurihara Sadako. *Genfukei o Idaite.* Tokyo, 1975.

Kurzman, Dan. *Day of the Bomb. Countdown to Hiroshima.* New York, 1986.

Lammers, Wayne P., and Osamu Masaoka. *Japanese A-Bomb Literature: An Annotated Bibliography.* Wilmington, DE, 1977.

Landstrom, Russell. *The Associated Press News Annual: 1945.* New York, 1946.

Lang, David. *From Hiroshima to the Moon.* New York, 1961.

Laurence, Bill. *Dawn over Zero. The Story of the Atomic Bomb.* New York, 1946.

————. *Men and Atoms.* New York, 1959.

Leahy, William D. *I Was There.* New York, 1950.

Lens, Sidney. *The Day Before Doomsday: An Anatomy of the Nuclear Arms Race.* Boston, 1978.

Lewin, Ronald. *The American Magic, Codes and Ciphers and the Defeat of Japan.* Middlesex, 1983.

Liebovich, Louis. *The Press and the Origins of the Cold War 1944–1947.* New York.

Liebow, Averill A., *Encounter with Disaster. A Medical Diary of Hiroshima, 1945*. New York, 1970.

Lifton, Robert Jay. *Death in Life*. New York, 1967.

Livingston, Jon, Joe Moore, and Felicia Oldfather, eds. *Postwar Japan: 1945 to the Present*. New York, 1973.

Long, Gavin. *MacArthur as Military Commander*. London, 1969.

MacArthur, Douglas. *Duty, Honor, Country*. New York, 1964.

————. *Reminiscences*. London, 1964.

————. *Reports of General MacArthur*. Washington, DC, 1966.

————. *Revitalizing a Nation*. Chicago, 1952.

Manchester, William. *American Caesar. Douglas MacArthur 1880–1964*. London, 1964.

Martin, Edwin M. *Allied Occupation of Japan*. Stanford, 1948.

Marx, Joseph Laurance. *Nagasaki: The Necessary Bomb?* New York, 1971.

Matsuno Hideo. *Taiyo ga ochiru*. Nagasaki, 1973.

Matsuura Sozo. *Senryoka no genron danatsu*. Tokyo, 1969.

Matusow, Bernstein. *The Truman Administration. A Documentary History*. New York, 1966.

Mayer, S. L. *MacArthur*. London, 1971.

————. *MacArthur in Japan*. New York, 1973.

Mayo, Marlene J. "Civil Censorship and Media Control in Early Occupied Japan." In *Americans as Proconsuls: United States Military Government in Germany and Japan*, edited by Robert Wolf. Carbondale, 1984.

————. *Educational and Social Reform*. Norfolk, 1982.

Millis, Walter, and E. S. Duffield. *The Forrestal Diaries*. New York, 1951.

Mitchell, Richard H. *Censorship in Imperial Japan*. Princeton, 1983.

Montgomery, John D. Forced to Be Free. The Artificial Revolution in Germany and Japan. Chicago, 1957.

————. *The Purge in Occupied Japan*. Chevy Chase, 1954.

Moore, Ray A. "The Occupation of Japan as History: Some Recent Research." *Monumenta Nipponica* 36, 3 (1981).

————. "Reflections of the Occupation of Japan." *Journal of Asian Studies* 38 (1979).

————, ed. *Japan under American Rule*. Tokyo, 1981

Morgan-Witts, Max, and Gordon Thomas. *Ruin from the Air*. London, 1977.

Murakami Hyoe. *Japan. The Years of Trial 1919–1952*. Tokyo, 1983.

Nagai Takashi. *The Bells of Nagasaki*. Tokyo, New York, and San Fransisco, 1984.

————. *We of Nagasaki—The Story of the Survivors in an Atomic World*. New York, 1951.

Nakajima Kenzo, ed. *Living Hiroshima*. Hiroshima, 1948.

Nishi Toshio. *Unconditional Democracy: Education and Politics in Occupied Japan 1945–52*. Stanford, 1982.

Nishimura, Sey. "Medical Censorship in Occupied Japan 1945–1948." *Pacific Historical Review* 58, 1 (February 1989).

Oe Kenzaburo. *Hiroshima Notes*. Tokyo, 1981.

Okuizumi Eizaburo and Jun Furukawa. "Nippon senryoku no kyokuto beigun joho shushu katsudo to soshiki." *Tokyo keizai daigaku gakkukaishi*, no. 109 (December 1978).

————, comps. and eds. *User's Guide to the Microfilm Edition of Censored Periodicals 1945–1949*. Tokyo, 1982.

Oppler, Alfred C. *Legal Reforms in Occupied Japan—A Participant Looks Back*. Princeton, 1975.

Pacific War Research Society. *Japan's Longest Day*. New York, 1968.

Passin, Herbert. "Japan and the H-Bomb." *Bulletin of Atomic Scientists* (October 1955).

Perry, John C. *Beneath the Eagle's Wings—Americans in Occupied Japan*. New York, 1980.

Phillips, Cabell. *The Truman Presidency: A History of a Triumphant Succession*. New York, 1966.

Price, Willard. *The Japanese Miracle and Peril.* New York, 1971.

Rose, Leslie A. *Roots of Tragedy: The United States and the Struggle for Asia 1945–53*. Westport, 1976.

Roth, Andrew. *Dilemma in Japan*. Boston, 1945.

Sakamoto Yoshikazu et al., comps. *Nihon senryo bunken mokuroku*. Tokyo, 1972.

Sasamoto Yukuo. "Genbaku higaishodo chosa ni okeru nihongun no yakuwari." *Rekishi to shakai*, no. 9 (1989).

Schaller, Michael. *The Origins of the Cold War in Asia: The American Occupation of Japan*. Oxford, 1985.

Schmidt, Benno. *Freedom of the Press vs. Public Access*. New York, 1976.

Schnabel, James F. *The History of the Joint Chiefs of Staff*. Washington, DC, 1979.

Schonberger, Howard. *Aftermath of War. Americans and the Remaking of Japan, 1945–1952*. Kent, 1989.

————. "The Japan Lobby in American Diplomacy 1947–1952." *Pacific Historical Review* 46 (1977).

Selden, Kyoko and Mark, eds. *The Atomic Bomb: Voices from Hiroshima and Nagasaki*. Armonk, NY, 1989.

Sherwin, Martin J. *A World Destroyed—The Atomic Bomb and the Grand Alliance*. New York, 1975.

Shimizu Hayao. "The War and Japan: Revisionist Views." *Japan Echo* 11 (1984).

Shulman, Frank, and Robert Ward. *The Allied Occupation of Japan. An Annotated Bibliography of Western Language Materials*. Chicago, 1974.

Smith, Alice Kimball. *A Peril and a Hope: The Scientists' Movement in America 1945–47*. Chicago, 1965.

Smith, Alice Kimball, and Charles Weiner, eds. *Robert Oppenheimer: Letters and Recollections*. New Haven, 1980.

Smyth, Henry D. *Atomic Energy for Military Purposes (The Smyth Report)*. Washington, DC, 1945.

Sodei Rinjiro. *Makkasa no nisen nichi*. Tokyo, 1974.

Soka Gakkai and *Japan Times. Cries for Peace—Experiences of Japanese Victims of World War II*. Tokyo, 1978.

Stimson, Henry L., and MacGeorge Bundy. *On Active Service in Peace and War*. New York, 1948.

Strauss, Lewis L. *Men and Decisions*. New York, 1962.

Sugimoto Yoshio. "Equalization and Turbulence: The Case of the American Occupation of Japan." Ph.D. dissertation, University of Pittsburgh, 1973.

Sumimoto Toshio. *Senryo hiroku*. Tokyo, 1952.

Svensson, Eric H. F. *The Military Occupation of Japan: The First Years. Planning, Policy Formulation and Reforms*. Denver, 1966.

Szilard, Leo. *Reminiscences. A Personal History of the Bomb*. Chicago, 1949.

Takakuwa Kokichi. *MacArthur no shimbun kenetsu—keisai kinen. Sakujo ni natta kiji*. Tokyo, 1984.

Takamae Eiji. *GHQ*. Tokyo, 1983.

――――. "The United States Occupation Policies for Japan." *Tokyo University Journal of Law and Politics* 14-5-13 (1973).

Takeshima Kazu. "Senryoki no kenetsu to hoso." NHK Report on Broadcast Research. Tokyo, December 1979.

Teller, Edward, with Allen Brown. *The Legacy of Hiroshima*. Westport, 1975.

Textor, Robert. *Failure in Japan*. New York, 1971.

Thomas, Donald. *A Long Time Burning. The History of Literary Censorship in England*. London, 1969.

Thorpe, Elliott R. *East Wind, Rain. The Intimate Account of an Intelligence Officer in the Pacific 1939–1949*. Boston, 1969.

Togo Shigenori. *The Cause of Japan*. New York, 1956.

Toland, John. *The Rising Sun—The Decline and Fall of the Japanese Empire 1936–1945*. New York, 1970.

Truman, Harry S. *Memoirs. Year of Decision*. Garden City, 1955.

Trumbull, Robert. *Nine Who Survived Hiroshima and Nagasaki*. Tokyo, 1957.

Uchikawa Yoshimi. "Nippon no hoso seisaku." *Studies of Broadcasting NHK*, nos. 6, 11.

Urata Minoru. *Senryogun no yubinkenetsu 1945–49*. Tokyo, 1969.

Vilkuna, Kustaa. *Sanan Valvonta—sensuuri 1939–1944*. Helsinki, 1962.

Vining, Elizabeth Gray. *Windows for the Crown Prince*. New York, 1952.

Wakefield, Harold. *New Paths for Japan*. London, 1948.

Ward, Robert E., and Yoshikazu Sakamoto, eds. *Democratizing Japan. The Allied Occupation*. Honolulu, 1987.

――――. *Policy and Planning during the Allied Occupation of Japan*, 1981.

Whitney, Courtney. *MacArthur: His Rendezvous with History*. New York, 1955.

Wilcox, Robert K. *Japan's Secret War: Japan's Race against Time to Build Its Own Atomic Bomb*. New York, 1985.

Williams, Justin. "Completing Japan's Political Reorientation, 1947–1952: Crucial Phase of the Allied Occupation." *American Historical Review* 73 (1968).

Willoughby, Charles. *MacArthur 1941–1951. Victory in the Pacific*. New York, 1954.

————, ed. *Supreme Commander for the Allied Powers*. Volume 1 Supplement: *MacArthur in Japan*. Washington, DC, 1966.

Wittner, Lawrence S. "MacArthur and the Missionaries. God and Man in Occupied Japan." *Pacific Historical Review* 40 (1971).

Wyden, Peter. *Day One. Before Hiroshima and After*. New York, 1984.

Yoshida Mitsuru. *Requiem for Battleship Yamato*, trans. Richard H. Minear. Tokyo, 1985.

INDEX

Monica Braw received her Ph.D. in history from the University of Lund, Sweden. She began covering Asia as a journalist in 1969, and since 1984 she has been the East Asia correspondent of the Swedish newspaper *Svenska Dagbladet*. Dr. Braw has written eleven books, including books on China and Japan as well as novels and short story collections, and her works have been published in Swedish, Finnish, German, English, and Japanese.